I0211882

FOREVER AND EVER is a collection of devotional poems—hymns of praise and somber elegies—written in 1952 and 1953 and dedicated to Adolf Hitler.

FOREVER AND EVER is one of three books left unpublished when Savitri Devi died in 1982. The manuscript was long thought to be lost. But in 2006, a French friend of Savitri contacted the Savitri Devi Archive with the news that all three volumes were extant.

FOREVER AND EVER is the first of Savitri Devi's long-awaited posthumous works to be published.

This volume also includes an additional poem, "In Memory of May 1st, 1945," written in 1946 by Clara Sharland, which is probably a pen name of Savitri Devi.

The Savitri Devi Archive

The Centennial Edition of Savitri Devi's Works
R. G. Fowler, General Editor
(Each volume will be released in a limited cloth edition of 200 numbered copies.)

Volume One:
AND TIME ROLLS ON
THE SAVITRI DEVI INTERVIEWS

Volume Two:
GOLD IN THE FURNACE
EXPERIENCES IN POST-WAR GERMANY

Volume Three:
FOREVER AND EVER
DEVOTIONAL POEMS

Volume Four:
DEFIANCE
THE PRISON MEMOIRS OF SAVITRI DEVI

Volume Five:
THE LIGHTNING AND THE SUN
(complete and unabridged)

Future Volumes:

PILGRIMAGE

MEMORIES AND REFLECTIONS OF AN ARYAN WOMAN

THE LOTUS POND
IMPRESSIONS OF INDIA

HARD AS STEEL

LONG-WHISKERS AND THE TWO-LEGGED GODDESS
OR, THE TRUE STORY OF A "MOST OBJECTIONABLE NAZI" AND . . .
HALF-A-DOZEN CATS

IMPEACHMENT OF MAN

A SON OF GOD
THE LIFE AND PHILOSOPHY OF AKHNATON, KING OF EGYPT
(complete and unabridged)

AKHNATON'S ETERNAL MESSAGE
(and other writings on Akhnaton)

A WARNING TO THE HINDUS
(and THE NON-HINDU INDIANS AND INDIAN UNITY)

NOT "FOR NOTHING": LETTERS OF SAVITRI DEVI, VOLUME 1

SAINT SAVITRI: LETTERS OF SAVITRI DEVI, VOLUME 2

SAVITRI DEVI

FOREVER & EVER

DEVOTIONAL POEMS

EDITED BY R. G. FOWLER

A Savitri Devi Archive Book
Counter-Currents Publishing, Ltd.
San Francisco
2021

Copyright © 2021

All rights reserved

Cover designed by Kevin Slaughter

ISBNs:
Hardcover: 978-1-64264-169-1
Paperback: 978-1-64264-170-7

Second Edition

To A. H.

"Wenn alle untreu werden,
So bleiben wir doch treu . . ."[1]

---

[1] "When everyone betrays you, we will still be true . . ." This is the first line of "Wenn alle untreu werden," also known as the "Treuelied" (Song of Faith) and the "S.S. Lied" — Ed.

CONTENTS

ILLUSTRATIONS

EDITOR'S PREFACE

Forever and Ever is Savitri Devi's volume of devotional and autobiographical poems dedicated to Adolf Hitler.

In Part I, Days of Growth, the first poem, "1918" focuses on the end of World War I; "1919" explores Savitri's alienation from modernity and longing for pagan Antiquity; "1923" commemorates Hitler's Beer Hall *Putsch*; "1929" tells the story of Savitri's pilgrimage to the Holy Land and her break with Christianity; and "1932" narrates her first journey to India. All of these events are also described in Savitri's other books, particularly *And Time Rolls On*.[1]

In Part II, Days of Glory, "1933" commemorates Hitler's attainment of power; "1935" is a composite description of one of the Nuremberg Rallies, based primarily on the Rally of 1934 as depicted in Leni Riefenstahl's documentary *Triumph of the Will*, released in 1935; "1938" tells of Savitri's work for the Hindu Mission; "1940" deals primarily with Hitler's defeat of France; "1942" focuses on the Japanese offensives in the Pacific and Far East. (The last three episodes are described in greater detail in *And Time Rolls On*.[2])

In Part III, Days of Horror, "1945" deals with the end of World War II and reveals that in her despair, Savitri had considered suicide; "1946" focuses on Savitri's return to Europe (also described in *Long-Whiskers and the Two-Legged Goddess* and *And Time Rolls On*[3]); "1948" tells of her propaganda missions in Occupied Germany (related in greater detail in *Gold in the Furnace* and *And Time Rolls On*[4]); "1949" describes her time in Werl

---

[1] Savitri Devi, *And Time Rolls On: The Savitri Devi Interviews*, ed. R. G. Fowler (Atlanta: Black Sun Books, 2005), ch. 1, "Autobiography," pp. 1–25.

[2] *And Time Rolls On*, pp. 24–39.

[3] Savitri Devi, *Long-Whiskers and the Two-Legged Goddess, or the true story of a "most objectionable Nazi" and . . . half-a-dozen cats* (Calcutta: Savitri Devi Mukherji, 1965), ch. 6, "Heliodora's Homeward Journey." *And Time Rolls On*, pp. 39–44.

[4] Savitri Devi, *Gold in the Furnace: Experiences in Post-War Germany,*

Prison after she was arrested, focusing specifically on her friend-
ship with Hertha Ehlert (for more details, see *Defiance* and *And
Time Rolls On*[5]); "1951" tells of her reactions to the execution of
seven Germans convicted of war crimes, the last executions of
this kind (for more details, see *Pilgrimage*[6]); the final poem,
"1953," ends the volume on a hopeful note, in the certainty that
the present Dark Age will be followed by a new Golden Age, in
accord with the cyclical laws of decay and rebirth.

Little is known about the composition of *Forever and Ever*. But
in *And Time Rolls On*, Savitri tells how she came to write "1953":

> In 1953, before I went back to Germany, I stayed for some
> time in Greece, and it was the birthday of a *Kameradin*
> whom I had met in Werl, a so-called war criminal, Her-
> tha Ehlert. . . . She was born on the 26th of March, 1905. It
> was the 26th of March, and I was in Athens. I was free,
> under the sunshine. She, poor thing, was in Werl still.
> She only came out later. And I went into a place where
> you get yogurt, and you can eat cakes and things like
> that. I had something to eat there. And it came to me. I
> thought of Hertha. I thought of her. I thought of her. And
> it came to me to write this poem.[7]

Finished in Athens on 26 March 1953, *Forever and Ever* was
written after *Defiance*, before *Pilgrimage*, and during the compo-
sition of *The Lightning and the Sun*, Part III, which deals with
Akhnaton.

In *Pilgrimage*, Savitri describes the ritual by which she con-
secrated the manuscript of *Forever and Ever* and other works on
30 October 1953 in the Chamber of the Sun at the Externsteine:

---

ed. R. G. Fowler (Atlanta: The Savitri Devi Archive, 2006). *And Time
Rolls On*, pp. 47–52.

[5] Savitri Devi, *Defiance: The Prison Memoirs of Savitri Devi*, ed. R. G.
Fowler (Atlanta: The Savitri Devi Archive, 2007). *And Time Rolls On*,
pp. 52–69.

[6] Savitri Devi, *Pilgrimage* (Calcutta: Savitri Devi Mukherji, 1958),
ch. 5, "Landsberg am Lech."

[7] *And Time Rolls On*, p. 170.

. . . I stretched out my arm and prayed: "Help me to contribute efficiently and lastingly to the resurrection, triumph and expansion, and definitive establishment of National Socialism in Germany, in the West, in the world, wherever there are people of Aryan blood. Help me to hasten the coming of the time when the proud Swastika Flag shall again wave above these sacred Rocks; when these Rocks will be honoured as Germany's spiritual centre, and Germany,—the modern Saviour's Fatherland,— as the Holy Land of Nordic mankind, sacred to all Aryans! Help me to achieve this through all I think and feel; through all I say or refrain from saying; through all I do or shall do; through all I wrote; all I am writing; all I shall ever write; through all that which I *am!*"[8]

Forever and Ever is one of three manuscripts left unpublished at the time of Savitri Devi's death. Publication proved impossible because on 1 March 1974, while living in New Delhi, Savitri Devi was assaulted, robbed of her gold jewellery, and left for dead by the side of a road. Savitri had a very French (and very Indian) distrust of banks, so this jewellery represented virtually her entire life's savings.

Savitri had planned to use her jewellery to pay for the publication of four books: *Forever and Ever, Hart wie Kruppstahl* (*Hard as Krupp Steel*, a political-philosophical work begun in the Fall of 1961 and completed in August 1963), *Tyrtée l'Athenien* (*Tyrtaios the Athenian*, a novel written in the mid-1960s), and *Souvenirs et réflexions d'une Aryenne* (*Memories and Reflections of an Aryan Woman*, a summation of Savitri's worldview begun in 1968 and completed on 12 September 1971).

Savitri struggled for more than two years to raise the funds to publish *Souvenirs et réflexions*, but after that, the strictures of poverty and the debilities of old age combined to make it her last book.

When Savitri died in England on 22 October 1982, the typescripts of *Forever and Ever, Hart wie Kruppstahl*, and *Tyrtée l'Athenien* remained unpublished. Some tantalizing fragments

---

[8] *Pilgrimage*, p. 352.

came to light during my research: Multiple copies of "1953," the final poem of *Forever and Ever*, were found in Savitri's correspondence. She also recorded it in the 1978 interviews that became *And Time Rolls On*. A couple of quotes from "1945" appear in letters to George Lincoln Rockwell (4 January 1961 and 28 August 1965). The table of contents and an English translation of the Epilogue of *Hart wie Kruppstahl* were among Savitri's correspondence with George Lincoln Rockwell. And, on 14 September 2004, I discovered the typescript of two chapters of *Tyrtée* and part of a third in the papers of Miriam Hirn, Savitri's literary executor. But as far as I knew, the rest of these books was simply lost.

I was, therefore, elated on 13 April 2006 when the Archive received word that the three "lost" works were extant in France in the hands of Savitri's friend Jean Rémy.

On 1 September 2006, the Archive received a photocopy of a typescript of *Forever and Ever*. I will refer to this as Typescript B. In my excitement, I announced in the front of my new edition of *Gold in the Furnace* that *Forever and Ever* would be the next volume (volume 3) in the Centennial Edition of Savitri Devi's Works.

However, as I transcribed and edited Typescript B, I noticed a number of sentences that made no sense. These sentences were not merely missing a word or two, for it is easy to make sense of such omissions. Thus I concluded that Typescript B, which had very few corrections, was a "fair copy" of another typescript, which I will call Typescript A. I hypothesized that when Typescript A was copied, the typist had to look back and forth between it and the typewriter, and as she did so, she dropped entire lines.

Furthermore, the "prose" version of "1953" included with Typescript B seemed to have been from another typescript. First, unlike Typescript B, in which there was a line typed below each title, this chapter had lines typed above and below the title. Second, unlike Typescript B, there were numerous hand-corrections.

The "verse" version of "1953" that came with Typescript B seems to have been typed separately from both typescripts, as the pages are numbered 1–3, whereas in both typescripts, it would have begun on page 63. I have included it here because it apparently was composed at the same time as the "prose" version, from which it differs little, and because it differs in a number of ways from the later version of "1953" which is published in *And Time Rolls On* as chapter 5.

I suspended work on *Forever and Ever* until I could get a copy of Typescript A and turned my attention to editing *Defiance*. When I received a copy of Typescript A on 30 August 2007, I found that my hypothesis was confirmed. The lacunae in Typescript B were significant and corresponded to entire lines in Typescript A, which were dropped by the typist making the copy. Economic necessities of my own, however, made it impossible for me to return to working on *Forever and Ever* until Winter–Spring of 2010, and my labours since then have been slow and intermittent.

This edition of *Forever and Ever* is a synthesis of Typescripts A and B. Typescript A is closest to the definitive version for two reasons. First, it is the most complete. Second, although most of the hand-corrections on Typescript A were typed into Typescript B, some hand-corrections on Typescript A were likely done *after* Typescript B was produced. (The typed texts are the same, but in Typescript A some words are altered by hand.) Alternatively, Savitri may simply have overlooked or intentionally omitted certain hand-corrections to Typescript A when she prepared Typescript B. However, some of the changes in Typescript B were systematic and thus deliberate, so I retained these. Where it was not clear if changes were intentional or not, my choice of versions was guided by my own taste.

If Savitri Devi had a chance to publish *Forever and Ever*, it surely would have been slightly different, judging from the many small changes she made to her favourite chapter "1953," which she distributed in handwritten form to her correspondents and friends throughout her life.

My goal has been to produce the best edition possible based on the extant texts. If the reader wishes to second-guess my choices, I have noted all variants and enclosed added words and punctuation in square brackets. Furthermore, PDF files of both typescripts are available online at The Savitri Devi Archive, http://www.savitridevi.org/.

Beyond combining the two typescripts, I made the minimum number of editorial interventions necessary to bring *Forever and Ever* into accord with today's standards. I corrected all spelling errors following Savitri's British English. I also updated her spelling, e.g., "for ever," "to-day." I preserved her sometimes eccentric capitalization and punctuation practices, although sometimes I quietly dropped a superfluous comma. I translated German quotations from *Mein Kampf* and provided citations. Finally, where useful, I have provided explanatory footnotes. Unless otherwise noted, all footnotes are mine.

The subtitle, *Devotional Poems*, is my own.

ACKNOWLEDGEMENTS

I wish to thank those friends of Savitri Devi and/or of the Savitri Devi Archive who helped make this book possible. First and foremost is Jean Rémy, who preserved Savitri's typescripts of *Forever and Ever* and made copies of them for the Archive. He also provided the image from Savitri Devi's 1940–1950 British Passport. Special thanks are also due Savitri's friend Miriam Hirn, who provided the typescript of "In Memory of May 1st, 1945" and most of the photo illustrations. I thank Beryl Cheetham for the picture of Hertha Ehlert that appears on page 87; D. A. R. Sokoll, for carefully reading the page proofs and spotting numerous errors, particularly in German; eagle-eyed proof-readers Matthew Peters and Larry C.; Matt Koehl of New Order for George Lincoln Rockwell's correspondence with Savitri Devi; and Michael J. Polignano for executing the first edition's cover and Kevin Slaughter for the second edition's cover.

I dedicate this book to the memory of Jean Rémy for his faithful friendship to Savitri and his responsibility to history.

R. G. Fowler
22 October 2010, revised 19 June 2021

FOREVER & EVER

FOR EVER AND EVER.....

by SAVITRI DEVI

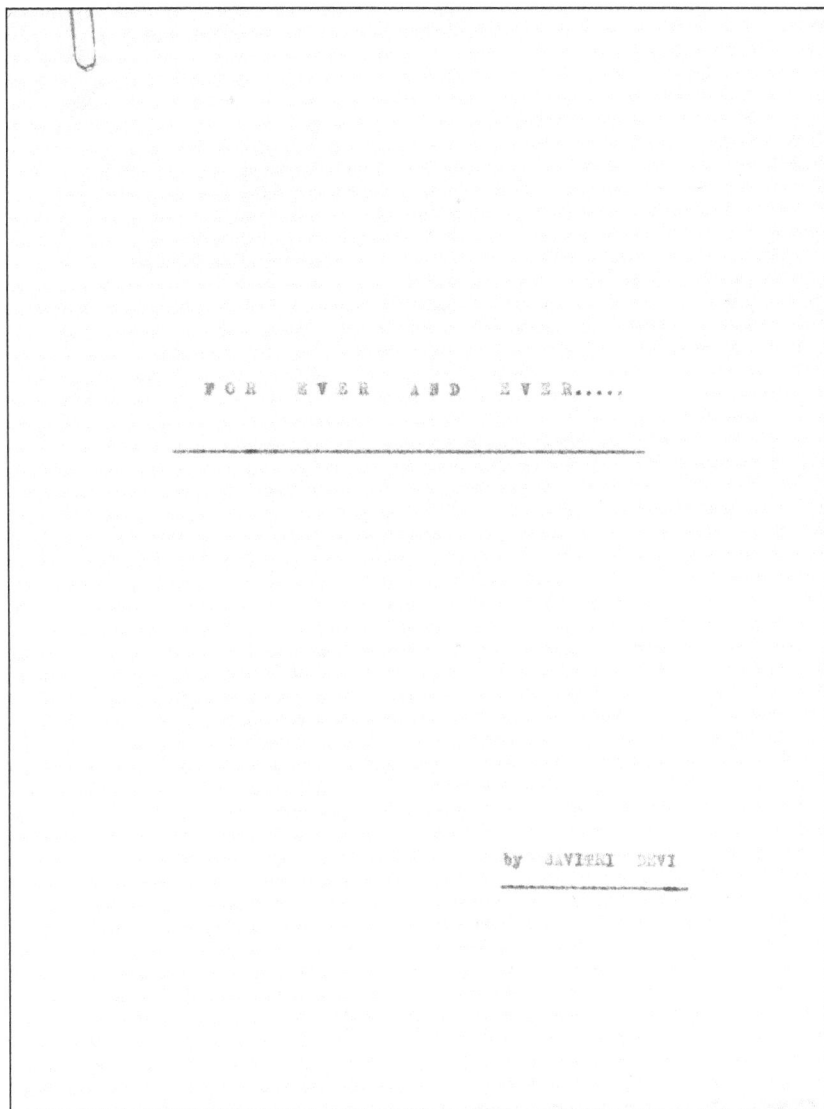

1. Cover page of FOREVER AND EVER, from Typescript A

Part One
DAYS OF GROWTH

2. Title page of Part One of FOREVER AND EVER, from Typescript A

3. Maximine Portaz, June 1918, age 12

Chapter 1

1918

"Es war also alles umsonst gewesen.
Umsonst all die Opfer und Entbehrung-
en, umsonst der Hunger und Durst von
manchmal endlosen Monaten, vergeblich
die Stunden, in denen wir, von Todes-
angst umkrallt, dennoch unsere Pflicht
taten, und vergeblich der Tod von zwei
Millionen, die dabei starben."

—*Mein Kampf*[1]

Hail, Thou exalted One, Whom I have never seen; maker of a
new world—my Leader!

From the dawn of Time, in ceaseless aspiration, I sought Thee,
I, the undying Soul of higher mankind, strong and fair. I
sought Thee in exile, and slavery and shame, unable to forget
the glorious destiny befitting me in spite of all. From age to
age, along the path that leads to certain death, I turned around
to contemplate an everlasting dream; and all my being leaped
towards the Saviour and the Lord Who was not there, but Who
would come, one day, and set me free, and give me back the

---

[1] "So it was all in vain. In vain all the sacrifices and privations, in
vain the hunger and thirst of sometimes endless months, in vain the
hours in which, gripped by mortal fear, we nevertheless did our duty,
and in vain the death of two million, who died that way" (*Mein Kampf*
[Munich: Franz Eher, 1939], pp. 223–24, trans. R. G. Fowler).

wings of youth; towards Thee, beloved Leader, Whose name no one yet knew.

When wouldst Thou come? Hundreds of years rolled by; new Kingdoms rose and fought, and in the mist[2] of time, slowly withered away; and gods changed names. One thing remained: the unpolluted stream of divine blood within the veins of the Gods' chosen people,[3] and the dim consciousness in these of a great duty to fulfill. When wouldst Thou come? From age to age, in the deep slumber of prosperity, again and again I called Thee. But the bright sky was deaf and dumb.

When once more all was lost, when all lay in the dust, when songs of hate echoed across the sacred Rhine, then didst Thou come — unknown; alone; out of the millions who awaited Thee; just one of them and nothing more, apparently; but one of them in whom[4] the betrayed gods of Aryandom lived and suffered and shone; one of them in Whose voice, the voice of the exalted Race of heroes dead in vain was soon to speak; and one in Whom the chosen lords of Earth, brothers of the immortal Youth, Baldur the Fair, were soon to hail their own invincibility. My Leader — our Leader — Thou wast there, somewhere, unnoticed, on a bed of pain. But it was not the torment of the body — the maddening torture of Thy burning eyes, blinded by poisonous gas; — it was not even the atrocious threat of possible unending night, that gripped Thy heart in agony. It was the news of the betrayal of Thy country, the humiliation of surrender, and the thought of all those who had died in vain in four long years. Oh, how the vision of their day-to-day dutiful sacrifice haunted Thy sleepless nights!

Thou laidst in mental agony a thousand times more horrid than any torture of the flesh. And from Thy blinded aching eyes, tears of powerless rage, tears of shame inexpressible, of

---

[2] Omitting a comma absent in Typescript A and present in Typescript B.

[3] Substituting "people" with "few" in accord with hand-correction to Typescript B.

[4] Omitting commas marking off "in whom."

boundless love and hate, rolled forth. No heart was torn as Thy great heart over the tragic fate of the millions whose blood was Thine — and mine; for indeed it is the same: Aryan blood.

Out of hunger and strife and devilish deceit, a new tremendous Power was taking shape in the bleak East. While on both sides of the Atlantic Ocean, the entire West, in childish glee, danced to the sound of drunken tunes, insulting Thy defeated people. Thou heardst the echo of their merriment; there, on Thy bed of pain.[5] Thou feltst the knife-thrust of their spiteful gaiety hundreds of miles away, while all round Thee Thou couldst but see Thy people's hunger and despair, and bitterness in harsh revolt against an unjust fate, against the accusing lies of a whole world.

And at that feeling, and at that sight, Thy ardent, bleeding heart aches with more love and with more hate — love for Thy martyred Nation, Thy greater Self, Whose life mattered alone; fathomless love, to which no sacrifice would ever be too great, no price too high if it could buy freedom and resurrection; hate for the workers of disaster, for those aliens whose cunning and whose wealth had long deceived and bribed the whole ignorant world, and turned the West against the best of its own flesh and blood.

And love and hate made Thee the Man who was to be — the Leader long awaited. The world was soon to see, through Thee, Thy people free; through Thee, the chosen blood protected and united within the growing Realm; through Thee, the god-like youth marching along the highways,[6] with songs of conquest, in the morning sun.

But I, Thy follower, Thy worshipper to be, Thy seeker through the gloom of Time, had not yet heard Thy name. Not far beyond the moving frontiers of the Realm, I awaited Thee unknowingly, deeming myself to be a thirteen-year-old maiden, while many centuries of age indeed I was; while before my

---

[5] This sentence is omitted in Typescript B.

[6] A comma appears in Typescript A, a semicolon in Typescript B.

dark eyes, fair shadows of a radiant past appeared and disappeared, reminding me of a forgotten world; foretelling me the glory of Thy great world to come.

And to the ugly crowd of liars and of cowards, I turned my back instinctively. Not even for a second did I feel happy as I heard the bells of victory. *Their* victory; not mine — I could have said: *not ours.*[7] I knew Thee not. (Who knew Thee, then?) And I knew not Thy people. But at the news of their defeat, my heart was sad, as though[8] the triumph of their enemies were, in my eyes, the triumph of guile and treachery and above all, of sickening mediocrity — of all I hated in the world. I knew Thee not; and yet I sought Thee in my dreams. Thy great Idea was mine;[9] had been from the beginning, the very yearning of my lonely soul. I was already Thy disciple, and Thy lover and Thy worshipper . . .

---

[7] Italicized following hand-corrections to Typescript B.

[8] Omitting a comma following hand-corrections to Typescript B.

[9] A comma appears in Typescript A, a semicolon in Typescript B.

Chapter 2

1919

"Auch das hellenische Kulturideal soll
uns in seiner vorbildlichen Schönheit
erhalten bleiben. Man darf sich nicht
durch Verschiedenheiten der einzelnen
Völker die größere Rassegemeinschaft
zerreißen lassen. Der Kampf, der heute
tobt, geht um ganz große Ziele: eine
Kultur kämpft um ihr Dasein, die
Jahrtausende in sich verbindet und
Griechen- und Germanentum
gemeinsam umschließt."

— *Mein Kampf* [1]

But yet, I knew Thee not;[2] I knew not Thy great people. And I did not suspect what possibilities lay within them, in our times, under my eyes.

Weary of the silly, sickly world which I did know; full of contempt for the conceited nation[3] that laughs at everything she

---

[1] "We should also retain the Hellenic cultural ideal in its exemplary beauty. One must not allow the larger racial community to be torn apart by the differences between individual peoples. The fight which rages today revolves entirely around grand goals: a culture fights for its existence, which encompasses the millennia and includes Greece and Germany together" (*Mein Kampf*, p. 470, trans. R. G. Fowler).

[2] Replacing a comma with a semicolon.

[3] Savitri refers here to France, the nation of her birth and

cannot understand, and holds in horror all extreme, uncompromising faiths;—the nation that put forth the world-wide snare: the "rights of man," and hates obvious[4] authority and iron order backed by force of arms, while she adores the unseen slavery of the gullible mind to lies;—full of contempt, also, for the religion that teaches that other great lie:[5] "the dignity of every human soul,"[6] in the name of a god whom I had never loved,[7] I turned my eyes to far-gone days; to gods and to heroes long dead, whose names no longer stirred devotion in the hearts of men, I gave my heart. I wept because I could not bring them back to life again.

The vision of the ancient Rock—of the Acropolis, seat of Perfection,[8] white and golden beneath Attica's cloudless sky[9]—lived[10] in my memory. And along with it, I adored the beauty of the manly virtues of heroes like unto the Gods—whether of those who stormed immortal Troy, three thousand years ago, or of those no less[11] great, and no less[12] godlike, who, merely a century before the present day, struggled for Hellas' freedom, in mountain fastnesses and on the sea, under the banner of the Cross. And along with it, I worshipped the beauty of the holy North in by-gone days, before its racial pride had yielded to the

---

upbringing.

[4] Typescript A reads "glaring."

[5] Typescript A originally read "snare," but it was crossed out, and "lie" was substituted.

[6] Typescript A originally continued with the words "put forth," but they were crossed out.

[7] Savitri refers here to Christianity.

[8] Typescript A originally continued "everlastingly," but it is crossed out.

[9] Typescript A originally continued with the words: "against the unreal background of Hymettus, purple and pink, in the light of the setting Sun, or shining under ghostly phosphorescent moon-rays, in the starry night," but they were crossed out.

[10] Typescript A originally read "shone," but it was crossed out, and "lived" was substituted.

[11] Typescript A reads "equally."

[12] Typescript A reads "equally."

foreign god of meekness; the beauty of the conquering men—
my mother's ancestors—who, when[13] in a deafening roar, an
outburst of monstrous glee, the Sky[14] and the Sea challenged
each other's might, the tempest howled, the thunder growled,
and lightning tore the crumbling clouds, stood in their ships,
erect, and beat their shields in cadence, and answering[15] the
furious Voice of elemental Godhead, sang warrior-like hymns
to Odin and Thor.

Where were they now, those supermen? Where was the spirit of
my race, which lived in me? Where was I now to find men at the
hearing of whose songs my heart would beat? Men in whose
words I would detect the spell of pride and power? Whose
voice[16] I gladly would obey?—Men whom I could admire?

All round me I beheld nothing but credulous and kindly apes,
or—which is worse—pedantic apes, well-read, but without
thought and without faith,[17] without the urge to fight for
Something greater than themselves and than their narrow
"happiness"; Something for which *men*[18] fight, along their way
to supermanhood. And only in the scattered lines of a few
dreamers did I find an echo of my yearning. "Come, O thou
exile of the far-gone times[19]"; said one of these. "The axe has
felled the sacred trees; where swords once clattered, now, the
slave doth crawl and pray. And all the Gods have gone away.
Come to Them in the gleaming Walhall, where They await
thee!"[20]

And I, fourteen, and full of youthful ardour, full of the thirst for

---

[13] Typescript A repeats "who."

[14] Capitalizing "Sky" to match "Sea."

[15] Typescript A reads "in answer to."

[16] Deleting a comma.

[17] Typescript B reads simply "without faith."

[18] Emphasis in Typescript A but not Typescript B.

[19] Typescript A reads "days."

[20] Freely rendered from Leconte de Lisle, "Le Barde de Temrah,"
Poèmes barbares (Paris: Alphonse Lemerre, n.d,), p. 71.

sacrifices[21] for Something that would mean, to me, all that the Gods of Greece and of the ancient North then[22] meant; and I the daughter of the North and of the[23] Aegean all in one, afire with love for Someone Who, to me, would be the embodiment of resurrected Aryandom—Someone Whom I could deify—I knew thee not, and wept. I wept over the Gods who had departed[24] never more to return; over the fair-haired warriors in whom their spirit dwelt; over the beauty and virility of Aryan man, the pride of Aryan woman, wife and queen—mother of men.

Slowly, but steadily, yet Thou wast rising, appointed by those very Gods whom I adored; to lead higher mankind to glory and to death, and then, to greater glory still. In Thy visible garb, thirty years old wert Thou, eternal One, my Saviour. Already, above the noise of catastrophic changes that shook the world, Thy people heard Thy voice proclaim the message of Thy anxious love—Thy ultimatum to the Chosen Nation—: "Future or ruin!" Already, to their depth, Thy inspired words had stirred them. Already a few, bold, hard and true—young men of gold and steel—had risen at Thy call and given Thee their all, and sworn to Thee, with joy, life-long allegiance in absolute obedience.

And just as when, before the storm, the surface of the sea[25] still remains calm, and the sky blue, meanwhile in unsuspected heights, slowly, tremendous whirls appear gathering scattered water-drops into dark clouds ready to burst; and just when no sign of new eruption can be shown in or around their silent, empty craters, down, down, low down in untold depths within the burning bowels of slumbering volcanoes, the unseen molten basalt boils and roars and rises day by day; so, likewise at the call of Thy compelling love; so, likewise at the light of

---

[21] Typescript A reads "full of the thirst of sacrifice."

[22] Typescript A first read "now," but it was crossed out, and "then" was substituted.

[23] The "the" was accidentally omitted from Typescript B.

[24] The words "thee not, and wept. I wept over the Gods who had departed" were accidentally omitted from Typescript B.

[25] Typescript B contains a superfluous comma.

Thy inspired, star-like eyes, slowly the age-old manliness and pride and will to power were roused anew within the heart of thy unhappy Nation. And children became men[26] within a day; and young men heroes. And while the land still groaned under the heels of victors who had made it clear that theirs would be the final word, and theirs the future of the world; while every voice was silent, excepting theirs,[27] in the great councils of the day, in which silly humanity was told to put its hope, from the breasts of the chosen few burst forth the cry that echoes Thine: "Awake, O nation fated to proclaim the divine right of pure blood; fated to rise and rule: Germany awake!"

Oh, had I heard the martial cry — the call to resurrection — and had I also known that along the way of Light, I would be allowed to follow Thee! That I too was invited to the great sacrifice in honour of the dawn; to the great Feast of Life at which, expressing my own youthful yearning, minstrels would praise the Gods I loved in magnificent hymns; to the great processional march in which, I too, would bear a torch, and I too add my voice to the broadening chorus, and in which on my right and on my left, and all around me I would have, as comrades, nay, as brothers, real demi-gods of flesh and blood! Oh,[28] had I known thou wast the One whom I had sought from century to century, and Whom I was still seeking, in ardent adolescent dreams! And that Thou wouldst welcome in me, the daughter of the outer Aryan world of North and South; the first-fruits of the love and reverence of the whole Race for Thee, its Saviour, Thee its Leader, Thee its uncrowned King! Had I but known . . .

But greater ones than I knew Thee not yet.

---

[26] The words "the heart of thy unhappy Nation. And children became men" were accidentally omitted in Typescript B.

[27] The words "would be the final word, and theirs the future of the world; while every voice was silent, excepting theirs" were accidentally omitted from Typescript B.

[28] "Oh" is added in Typescript B.

Chapter 3

1923

(9th November)

"Am 9. November 1923, 12 Uhr 30 Min-
uten nachmittags, fielen vor der Feld-
herrnhalle sowie im Hofe des ehe-
maligen Kriegsministeriums zu Mün-
chen folgende Männer im treuen Glau-
ben an die Wiederauferstehung ihres
Volkes: . . .

"So widme ich ihnen zur gemeinsamen Er-
innerung den ersten Band dieses Werkes,
als dessen Blutzeugen sie den An-
hängern unserer Bewegung dauernd
voranleuchten mögen."

— *Mein Kampf* [1]

Then came a day when, confident in Thy increasing might, in
Thy devoted followers and in Thy Destiny, Thou stoodst in

---

[1] "On 9 November 1923, at 12:30 in the afternoon, in front of the
Feldherrnhalle and likewise in the courtyard of the former War Min-
istry in Munich, the following men fell in true faith in the resurrection
of their people: . . . Thus I dedicate the first volume of this work to the
common memory of them, its blood witnesses, may you shine on be-
fore the followers of our movement" (*Mein Kampf*, Dedication, trans.
R. G. Fowler).

broad daylight against the public powers, slaves of Thy peo-
ple's foes, challenging them in an unequal fight; a day when
boldly facing the threat of the existing State and its awe-
inspiring apparatus[2] of repression—its soldiery without ideas,
a tool in the hands of respectable authorities without a soul—
Thy few and fiery faithful ones marched forth to storm for Thee
the citadel of undisputed power.

Their countenances bright with joy, their hearts full of that
burning love that carries one to the ends of the earth and never
turneth backwards; Thy name upon their youthful lips, as in all
times to come, already linked inseparably with the holy name
of Germany, on they went without fear . . . Sunshine is beauti-
ful, daylight is sweet; and yet, more beautiful, and sweeter still,
is death for Thee, death for Thy great Idea to triumph; for Thy
reign to come.

On they went, and no force upon earth or in heaven could stop
the impetus of their conquering step; for theirs was Germany's
eternal soul after a long time wide-awake and free; theirs, the
message of truth, the spell of resurrection; and theirs, in spite of
all,—after the coming flash of power and of glory, and follow-
ing untold years of martyrdom—the lordship of the future;
theirs the world, in its new golden age, after the final crash.

On they went. On its topmost wave, the great unfurling tide of
History that none can alter or arrest, carried them to their fated
goal: to glory in unending time,—but first, to death. The rifles
of the wavering State went off, and bullets flew; and on the
ground, in pools of blood, lay sixteen men of those who were
the very best of Germany's best, Thy faithful ones of early
days, Thy chosen few, men of all trades and of all ranks (there
are no social ranks, among us who believe in the nobility of
Aryan blood alone),[3] men of all ages too, the oldest over fifty,
the youngest just nineteen, but all young men at heart, all look-
ing to the future, all men who firmly felt that, to begin anew,

---

[2] Reading "apparel" in Typescript A and B as "apparatus."
[3] Adding a comma.

and build in truth and fervour, trusting one's Nation's[4] fate, it is never too difficult, never too late.

In brotherly equality, in pools of blood they lay, the first ones of an endless list of martyrs of the Cause of Life in truth, under its modern form; the first to win the honour of giving up their lives for Thee and for new Germany, their resurrected Father-land—and Thine—and; beyond that, new Aryandom, Thy world-wide dream of beauty,—and mine.

There they lay, while the might that Thou wert soon to over-throw—the might of those authorities in the service of foreign wealth—gripped a few other of Thy trusted ones, and Thee Thyself, and led you all into captivity. On Thee, the heavy for-tress doors were shut for several months.

The newspapers mentioned the fact, mentioned also the death of the first martyrs. But outside Germany, few understood how great a happening had taken place; how great a new upheaval, in joyous sacrifice and death,[5] was taking shape.

As for me, on the tragic day on which the Sixteen fell for Thee, I was hundreds of miles away, standing alone upon the marble steps of the Parthenon, and gazing at the City at my feet, and at the distant[6] sea.

I was eighteen, and fair to look upon; yet no womanly sadness brought tears to my eyes. Ardent, but proud, and already be-fore this birth, marked out to love [none] but Godhead incar-nate, never was I to know the joys and anguishes of human passion, nor its madness.

I loved a dream, and tears were in my eyes because I was be-coming conscious that it was but a dream. I loved eternal Greece—that Greece of long ago, that survives in the lofty col-

---

[4] "Nation's" is omitted in Typescript B.
[5] Comma omitted in Typescript B.
[6] The words "distant the" are added in Typescript B. I deleted the superfluous "the."

umns within the shade of which I stood; also that Greece of yesterday, bulwark of Aryan mankind in the Near East, who, for five hundred years, resisted the victorious Turks. I loved the Prince of Macedon, the fair-haired Conqueror, whose march towards the East, resembled the procession of an irresistible god; the Man who led men of my race across the Indus River for the second time. I loved, also the Grecian chieftains who, in 1821, swore to reconquer freedom or to[7] die. And tears were in my eyes because of bitter thoughts.

All round me, in the dazzling midday light, my beloved Athens spread its white houses, in the midst of which, a few cypress trees here and there, and rows of pepper trees, put patches of dark green or lines of greenish gray; its white houses that covered the lower slopes of steep Lykabettus, up to the pine tree wood I knew so well. Beyond the outskirts of the town, towards the east, the barren rocks of Hymettus, in light, almost transparent gray, shone against the background of a blue sky that was so blue that it could seem unreal. And to the north, and to the west, I admired the sober outlines of other hills against[8] that same fathomless blue background; and, to the south, the sparking Aegean, bluer still—deep, violet-blue.

Oh, how beautiful it all was: that City, from a distance, so white in the sunshine, amidst its clear-cut hills, and, high above all, the everlasting sky; and far around all, the everlasting sea!

And yet, my heart was sad, for out of all that beauty, no Grecian voice had yet answered my fiery call to freedom,[9] my call to pride. None had agreed with me when I had said that worse than [the] Turkish yoke was slavery to the so-called "great" powers who had just won the First World War. And when, leaving the rest aside, I had recalled the latest blow of fate—the loss of Asia Minor—and had accused the treacherous Allies,

---

[7] The "to" is omitted in Typescript B.

[8] The words "the background of a blue sky that was so blue that it could seem unreal. And to the north, and to the west, I admired the sober outlines of other hills against" were omitted from Typescript B.

[9] "And" is added in Typescript B.

and had accused the spirit they embodied (the spirit of Democracy) and accused the alien interests behind their policy, and tried to prompt my brothers to have nothing to do with them and their soul-killing "culture," no one had seemed to share my burning indignation; none had echoed my hate.

Had Greece, then, irredeemably lost every sense of grandeur, and consented to be forever a tool of the western Allies, a docile instrument of their intrigues, exalted when it suited them, and the following day insulted and abandoned? Was she no longer to remain, in opposition to both Turk and Jew, the advanced guard of Aryandom? The treacherous Allies, by doing all they could to help the Turks to win the Asia Minor War, acted as enemies of Aryan blood. But why did not Greece hate them, as I did? Were not the flames of devastated Smyrna, was not the forced exile of two millions of Hellenes enough to stir, in her, that self-same disgust as I felt for those great money-ridden States that had, six years before, against her will, dragged her into their unjust war? Was all that not enough to make her say, with me: "Away! Away from that hypocrisy, which Democracy signifies![10] Away, away from the serfdom of the decaying West! And back to national values; back to the spirit of the national Gods of old, heralds of Life undying! Back to ourselves; to Hellenism, — to Aryandom!" (The two, in my eyes, were the same.)

These were my thoughts as, on the memorable Day, I stood upon the steps of the Temple in ruins, and beheld in its beauty, under the midday Sun, the violet-crowned City.

My Leader, had I then, but known the deeper meaning of Thy holy Struggle! Had I but understood that the Sixteen, whose death the papers of the following day stated within a line, had shed their blood for something more than a new form of government! Oh, had I seen in them, what they already were: the vanguard of an endless host of fighters for the rule of the natural elite of mankind, — the first ones in my times to die for my

---

[10] "Signifies" is replaced by "stands for" in Typescript B.

eternal Greek ideal of domination of the *aristoi*,—the best, in body, character and soul! And had I understood, that, in the modern world, the best, according to my heart's conception, according[11] to the everlasting standards of health, and strength, and beauty, set forth by my Greek masters, were the élite of Thy inspired countrymen: *Thy* best!

In youthful fervour, then and there, I should have flown to Thee![12]

Oh, why did I not know? In the heat of Thy struggle, I should have been so happy; I should have loved Thee so, from those great early days!

Yet, there I was, and Thine already in spirit, and by the Gods themselves chosen to remain Thine throughout a thousand wanderings. Why did I not guess? Who can tell? All-penetrating is the Gods' insight—and strange, and often disappointing, outwardly, are their ways.

4. Maximine Portaz, August 1923, age 17

---

[11] "According" is added in Typescript B.
[12] A paragraph break is inserted in Typescript B.

Chapter 4

1929

"So glaube ich heute im Sinne des
allmächtigen Schöpfers zu handeln: *In-
dem ich mich des Juden erwehre, kämpfe ich
für das Werk des Herrn.*"

—*Mein Kampf* [1]

I had never loved the Christian faith; indeed, its contempt of
the body, its stress upon the love of man, whichever man he
be,—while it forgets to teach love and respect of living Nature,
ever beautiful—its fear of healthy pride and violence,[2] and of
the joy of one[3] who needs no comfort in this world and no
hope outside,[4] had all, and from the start, made me despise it,
if not to hate it.

Yet, for long years, I had not known what open stand to take,
before the eyes of all, for or against it. For years,[5] I had tolerat-

---

[1] "Thus I now believe myself acting in accordance with the al-
mighty creator: *By defending myself against the Jew, I fight for the work of
the Lord*" (*Mein Kampf*, p. 70, trans. R. G. Fowler).

[2] In Typescript B the phrase "healthy pride and violence" is man-
gled as "healthy and violence pride."

[3] In Typescript B, "one" is replaced with "anyone."

[4] In Typescript B, "otherworldly hope" is replaced by "hope out-
side," probably to eliminate the repetition of "world."

[5] In Typescript B, "For years," is replaced by "And."

ed it,[6] solely because I had, over and over again, been told that, without it, the speech and soul of Greece would have perished wholesale during the long[,] long night of Turkish domination; because I knew that, before that, the Byzantine Empire bore for a thousand years the double stamp of Christendom and of Hellenic culture; also because I recognized, within the music of the Eastern Church, the last bond of allegiance of thousands of scattered exiles to the hellenic Nation, as well as an echo of I knew not what glory of a remoter past, of a more national existence, in the light of national Gods.[7]

I had tolerated it. But never could I love it. Never could I admire that meekness which it taught; nor that propensity to exalt the weak and sick in body or in spirit, the crippled and the unhappy, at the expense of those whom Nature cherishes: the healthy and the strong, the free and the all-round beautiful.[8] Nor could I share that tendency to ponder over lust and greed and every sin, delighting in perpetual repentance; that craving to seek out and save what in my eyes was not worth saving; that constant thought of a dull heaven coupled with a constant aspiration to the dust.

Whenever, from a distance, I beheld on the top of Areopagus, the church erected on the spot where the Jew taught, for the first time, in Athens, that "God hath made all men out of one blood,"[9] I felt my own blood boil with shame. "Oh, why, why had they listened to him, the proud Athenians of the old days?" thought I. And I remember the story of the conquest of tired Hellas by the foreign creed. It was not they, the people of the Goddess, who had harkened to the Jewish lie; it was the many ones of doubtful origin although of Grecian speech, who

---

[6] In Typescript B, "tolerated it" is repeated.

[7] In Typescript B, this reads, "also because, embodied in the music of the Greek Church, I felt the last bond of allegiance of thousands of scattered exiles to Greece and to her past, as well as an echo of I knew not what glory of a remoter past; of a more national existence, in the light of national Gods."

[8] Replacing a question mark with a period.

[9] An exclamation point is added in Typescript B.

formed the sweepings of Grecian seaports; it was also the men of Alexandria, and, above all, it was the policy of Constantine whom they called the "Great" that helped the new religion to take a hold in Greece, three hundred years after the death of Paul. And I remembered him, more and more dear to me, warrior-like Emperor Julian, who tried to stem the tide. And I recalled the words of despair he is said to have uttered on the battlefield, acknowledging the victory of the Christians, as he died.[10] And I recalled Hypatia torn to pieces; and also, for beyond the Greco-Roman[11] world, in that proud North, whose daughter I too was, for centuries on end, the trail of persecution of Aryan Heathendom by zealous Christian knights.

Just as, in this triumphant eastward march from victory to victory, fair Alexander had carried hellenic might to the hallowed Land of Seven Rivers, through the bright mountain Pass through which the earliest Aryan warriors had come there long before, so had, in the course of time, the sickly Jewish creed, avenging the defeat[s] of Gaza and of Tyre, conquering decaying Greece through bribery, and the pure-blooded, virgin North through terror. Its world-wide and lasting success was, in my eyes, the sign of the rise of lower mankind, against the strong, against the fair, against the Gods' own children, my people, whether from the shores of the Ionian Sea or of the German Ocean.

What link of sheer historical propriety still retained me within that Christendom, which I despised? And was that link a living fact? In spite of all the usefulness the Christian Church might well have had, in the dark Turkish days, were not the spirit of eternal Greece and that of the[12] Galilean faith forever incompatible? Did not, in spite of all, an abyss gape between them; in time and in eternity? And if so, had I not to choose, once and for all, which path was to be mine? I longed to feel, in its very

---

[10] *"Vicisti, Galilaee"* ("You have won, Galilean" — or, as it is usually rendered, "Thou hast conquered, Galilean").

[11] Deleting a superfluous comma.

[12] In Typescript B, a superfluous "of" is added.

birthplace, the soul of historic Christianity — to see, to hear, to know. I longed to let my eyes measure the breadth and the depth of that abyss I felt between myself and it.[13] And so, one April morning in 1929, upon a Christian pilgrims' ship, I sailed to Palestine.

5. Maximine Portaz, August 1925, age 19, wearing a crucifix

Upon the glimmering waves between the many golden isles, the ship carried me away from Greece, over many hundred miles; away from Greece, it took me straight into another world — into that old Semitic East where the Christian creed was born.

---

[13] In Typescript B, the phrase "my eyes measure the breadth and the depth of that abyss I felt between" is omitted.

And I beheld the Soul of the Semitic East, itself foreign to me, dominated and spoilt for centuries and centuries by the influence of those rejected ones of history, for whose unholy might and unseen rule my own decaying continent had toiled unknowingly, from those dark days it had embraced the Christian faith, and made the Christian values the basis of its whole outlook on life: the Jews. And I beheld the selfish, cunning, loveless Soul of Israel behind the serpentine courtesy of the men in long dark clothes who sold in the bazaars, no less than in the fanatical glances of the same ones, whose movements I followed, a few days later, before the Wailing Wall. And everywhere, in churches and in mosques, and in the malodorous[14] winding streets of old Jerusalem, where life has never changed, and in the new and vulgar brightly-lighted buildings of Tel Aviv; I saw the self-same stamp of that beautyless race; the self-same sign of mankind's fall. Even the nomad dweller in the Desert[15] had fallen at the contact of the Jew. He had slowly learnt from him to repudiate his age-old tribal pride, founded upon the brotherhood of blood, and to rejoice, instead, in the great unity of all the true believers, whoever these may be, and in their equal right to beget more believers in the Book—in the One God and in the Prophet—never mind by whom. And I thought: even the Bedouin have decayed; what about us, the children of the godlike men of distant midnight shores, who once[16] had brought the cult of Apollo to Greece and carried to India the worship of the Dawn? What about us, when our deluded fathers accepted from the Jew a creed upholding meekness, and charity towards all men and love of peace as virtues? A creed in which the body no longer mattered, and in which, as in Islam, the original ideal of pure blood was looked upon as obsolete?

I gazed at those who had come with me to Palestine—people from Greece—and I measured the distance that separated them from the Heathen Greeks of old, as I had never measured it be-

---

[14] Reading "malodorant" as "malodorous."

[15] In Typescript B, "in the Desert" is omitted.

[16] Deleting a superfluous comma.

fore. In some of them, under a skin-deep Christian faith, the eternal Soul of Greece still shone, invincible, and ever-ready to reassert itself. In others I beheld but Christian Levantines, product[s] of long decay. I suddenly recalled the dome of the great church erected to Saint Paul upon the top of Areopagus, under that same blue sky on the background of which the ruins of the old heathen Acropolis appear in all their untarnished splendour. All around me, that same oppressive style, so different from all that real Greece had created; all around me, that foreign atmosphere, that mysticism of the Semitic East, so different from the spirit of our cult of Rhythm and Form, of our cult of Health and Light—our Aryan cult, faithful to this fair earth. I shuddered at the contrast, more deeply than ever before. And from the inner feeling of my own everlasting Self, of my own Race, of which at last I was fully aware; and from the inner vision of my own dream of an ideal world, I formulated in my heart the long-delayed decision on which my whole life was to rest: "Away from Jewry! Away from the Christian spirit, the subtle poison poured out to us by the Jews, well-guided by the instinct of their race to emasculate our bodies and kill our Aryan pride! Away from all that, and back to what we would have been today, had Paul never set foot in Athens, or had divine Julian been able to arrest the overwhelming tide of darkness![17] No further compromise with a foreign tradition in the name of the memory of the Eastern Empire: Eternal Greece, and, beyond her, indestructible Aryandom of North and South—higher mankind—must pass before the lure of a mere thousand years of history."

Thus did I feel in those old churches built upon the famous spots holy to every Christian; in the monastery where I remained, and in the glittering mosque of Omar, that I visited, and in the streets of old Jerusalem, and on Mount Zion. Thus did I feel along the roads of Palestine, upon my way to towns and villages bearing biblical names.

Hundreds of miles away, among Thy blessed people, under

---

[17] In Typescript B "of darkness" is omitted.

Thy leadership, my dream was taking shape. And day by day, in hope and in increasing strength, in confidence and joy, Thy people were growing into a rising force.[18] And Thou wast waiting for the Day when that force[19] would break down the barrier within which the frightened world was trying in vain to keep it.

And I was soon to understand; and I was soon to admire Thee; and I was soon to love Thee, alone of all the sons of men in our times.

From far, within my heart, I watched the joyous[20] tide gain power. I admired its impetus, and recognized in it the Force that had once given Greece to the Aryan Race, and the broad[21] East to conquering Greece. Already, in the realm of the invisible, my life-long yearning met Thy masterful will-power, and paid to Thee the tribute that I was one day to express in words of burning faith; the lasting tribute of the brothers of Thy people from[22] the whole world — the love of the whole Race.

---

[18] In Typescript A, "tide" is crossed out and replaced by "force." In Typescript B, "tide" remains. This may mean that Typescript A was edited after the creation of Typescript B, or Savitri may simply have decided to ignore her hand-correction to Typescript A when she prepared Typescript B.

[19] In Typescript A, "tide" is crossed out and replaced by "force." In Typescript B, "tide" remains.

[20] "Joyous" is added by hand to Typescript A, but is not present in Typescript B.

[21] "Broad" is added by hand to Typescript A, but is not present in Typescript B.

[22] In Typescript B, "in" is replaced with "from."

Chapter 5

1932

"Alle großen Kulturen der Vergangen-
heit gingen nur zugrunde, weil die ur-
sprünglich schöpferische Rasse an
Blutvergiftung abstarb."

— *Mein Kampf* [1]

"Away, away to India; away to the hallowed country where the Aryan Gods have never died and need not be revived!" thought I. "Greece has become the prey of money-grabbing foreigners, and the victim of alien Gods and alien teachings; and I cannot do anything to awake her sleeping soul; over and over again her children have reminded me that I am nobody and that my voice has no echo in any heart.

"In resurrected Germany, no doubt, the everlasting spirit of the best people of my race is growing day by day more powerful; and *He* is there. But would *He* really welcome *me*, an Aryan from abroad, as one entirely his own? Would his people believe me when I say that I love and admire them? In my own land nobody has believed me yet. No; better be a foreigner in a far-away land,—a western Aryan Heathen in the last citadel of Aryan culture in the East—rather than in the very midst of the one land in Europe where my own

---

[1] "All great cultures of the past perished only because the originally creative race died of blood poisoning" (*Mein Kampf*, p. 316, trans. R. G. Fowler.

spirit is rising day by day! So let me go! One day I shall come back."

Thus thought I as the ship sailed on, further and further south, — down the Red Sea, — and carried me I knew not where nor for how long. Standing alone upon the deck, I watched the innumerable stars in the dark sky and, now and then, as I cast down my eyes, the phosphorescent circles of innumerable jellyfish in the dark waters. Gliding between the two gorgeous infinities, I felt my nothingness but also realized the ineffable tuning of all my being to the silent music of the Universe. My unsuspected destiny, I knew, was a detail in a huge Destiny by far transcending me. And all that I did had to be. And from the stars and from the depth of the dark shining waters, I felt the unseen Forces guiding me and carrying me (never mind through what wanderings) where I was bound to go: to the fulfillment of thousands of years of yearning; to the glory of a new youth in Thy new world — to Thee, the everlasting Friend; the One Who comes over and over again.

And every radiant dawn and every fiery sunset that I admired upon the sea, brought the world nearer the great blessed Day of Thy Seizure of Power, while I sailed further and further away from Europe — from Thy Realm. Further and further away[2] . . . yet, along my own path, nearer to the outlandish post from which my fate had willed that I should fight for Thee, forever nearer Thee in spirit, for Thy unseen and broader Realm extends above all boundaries to wherever Thy faith in Health and God-made Order, lives within Aryan hearts.

❖ ❖ ❖

I reached Aryavarta, the Land of many races, where teeming millions, to this day, honour the fair descendants of the

---

[2] The words "from Europe — from Thy Realm. Further and further away" were omitted from Typescript B.

ancient bards of my own race as gods on earth; where nei-
ther gold nor might, nor learning, nor anything that can be
bought and sold,[3] nor anything that man can conquer, but
purity of blood alone is treasured for six thousand years.

And then I saw the wondrous sight: Rameshwaram, the
temple erected by the faith of millions to the glory of the
fair immemorial Aryan hero, Rama, Conqueror of the
South. I saw its many-storied *gopurams* towering far above
the flimsy roofs and dusty crowded streets of the Dravidian
village in holy festive mood. And to the sound of music
never heard before, I passed under its doorway, I too
draped in bright silk, I too with jasmine flowers in my hair
like the daughters of India, I, the ambassador of distant
western Aryandom to the surviving stronghold of Aryan
faith in the Far South. And at the entrance, on the right and
on the left as though it were welcoming me, I saw, in
gleaming vermillion, the well-known Sign, the old Wheel of
the Sun — our Sign. And tears came to my eyes.

I walked along gigantic corridors, past endless rows of
stately pillars through which I could behold no end of halls,
more pillars and more corridors. My footsteps sounded
strange upon the pavement, and in the voice that sprung
from my own lips I could not recognize my voice. I wan-
dered in elation, as in a world of dreams. Music of flutes
and kettledrums resounded through the echoing halls, full
of the scent of burning incense and fresh flowers. Dusky
velvet-eyed men, all clad in white, and dusky women clad
in many colours and full of strange serpentine grace,
passed by like shadows. And suddenly night came — the
warm tropical night heavy with perfume and alive with
hunger and with lust, with the great life of forest and of
jungle. And the Full Moon of Vaishakha shone in the violet
sky, shedding its phosphorescent light over the mighty
towers and sculptured domes and outer walls and colon-

---

[3] The words "nor anything that can be bought and sold" were
omitted from Typescript B.

nades and over the still surface of the sacred tank, while growing darkness filled the halls and more offering-bearing crowds poured in from every doorway. And I stayed on and on—to watch, to feel, to know the Feast of living Aryan Heathendom in a strange land; the homage of the conquered South to the deified northern Warrior and King, Rama, now, in our times, after thousands of years.

And then, out of the[4] darkness came the blast of music and the thundering throbs of drums, and light appeared,—the light of burning torches held by a hundred men. And, suddenly, in the light, I saw a row of sacred elephants emerge in glittering array; seven of them, with ritual stripes of vermillion and sandal[wood] paste upon their massive foreheads, and scarlet cloths with golden fringe hanging down from their towering backs. The processional chariot of Rama and of Sita followed, covered with flowers by the handful on its passage.[5] And the red glow of torches shone upon the dusky faces, many of which were regular and beautiful. And the half-naked youths who drove the elephants and those who bore the torches seemed as though they were likenesses of Grecian gods in living bronze.

I watched them pass; I watched them go, further and further away along the echoing pillared corridors and around the moonlit sacred tank. And for the second time my eyes were filled with tears. For in a flash my mind went back to Europe where I had so many times and for so long dreamed with nostalgic sadness of that unbroken Pagan ritual; to Europe where, I knew, Thou[6] wast calling Thy people to a new rising of the Aryan spirit, nay to the birth in them of a new Aryan soul, with all the decorous display and all the pomp that young creative faith could put forth when allied to the spontaneous love of order and of beauty. I thought of

---

[4] The words "depth of" are omitted from Typescript B.

[5] In Typescript A, this reads ". . . covered with flowers. The crowd cast flowers by the handful on its passage."

[6] Capitalizing "thou."

other torch-processions in an entirely different setting—
processions[7] of the new rising Germanic creed of pride in
racial purity, in which the fire-bearers were tall, athletic
blond young men, sons of that hallowed North whence
long ago both Greece and India had drawn their noblest
blood and the new light that was to make them everlasting.
"At last, after so many centuries of demoralization through
the poison of Christian-like equality, the eternal values of
my race are again being upheld, in broad daylight on my
own continent," thought I, for the millionth time. "But why
had they ever been brushed aside? Why did the Jewish
teaching ever conquer our fathers?"

And all through these fifteen hundred long years, during
which Europe had been worshipping her Jewish god and
lowering herself before his priests, and exalting moral
standards of human brotherhood destined to give her very[8]
soul to Israel, here in the Tropics, so[9] far away, India's
dusky millions had clung most faithfully to Aryan gods;
here, when the moon was[10] full during the month of
Vaishaka, year after year men had come forth in crowds to
honour Rama, the Aryan conqueror of Ceylon; here,
throughout India's stormy history, through invasions and
through wars, and in spite of all the levelling creeds im-
ported by crusaders of equality and sneaking preachers of
humanity, the time-honoured caste hierarchy had pre-
served pure blood, and kept alive a handful of real Aryans;
here, every man, even among the lower races, believed in
racial hierarchy, and knew his place—believed in *our* prin-
ciples, in *our* faith, in *our* world New Order, without being
aware of it.

---

[7] The words "in an entirely different setting—processions" are
omitted from Typescript B.

[8] "Very" is omitted in Typescript B.

[9] "So" is omitted in Typescript B.

[10] Deleting a superfluous "in its" that appears after "was" in both
typescripts.

Around the moonlit sacred tank, slowly moved the procession. And one after the other, for a while, the intricately sculptured pillars were lighted up by [the] scarlet glow. And kettledrums and flutes and clashing cymbals mingled their deep vibrations and their high-pitched notes in deafening outlandish music under the luminous infinity of the sky. And coils of incense filled the air, — the offering of the South to the great Aryan hero, now, yesterday, and in all times, foreshadowing the future homage of varied races of all climes, the homage of the conquered world to the godlike Race; to Thee, my Leader, to Thy people; to the everlasting noble blood, fated to rule; both Thine . . . and mine.

I shut my eyes, and thought of the great miracle that Thou wast working far away: of the new Europe of our dreams. And amidst the solemn mystic roar that held me as though under a spell, that roar of joyous fervour, centuries old, — and amidst the smoke of incense and the jasmine breath of that bright southern night, untold elation filled my heart. And blending in a dream the age-old homage of the South, that I admired, with the tremendous hope of Thy power and glory, I thought, in an ecstatic smile: ". . . and tomorrow, the whole world!"[11]

---

[11] In Typescript A is a hand-written footnote: "'. . . und morgen die ganze Welt!' (Old Song)." The song is "Es zittern die morschen Knochen" ("The Rotten Bones Tremble") a.k.a. "Wir werden weiter marschieren" ("We Will March On") by Hans Baumann.

Part Two
DAYS OF GLORY

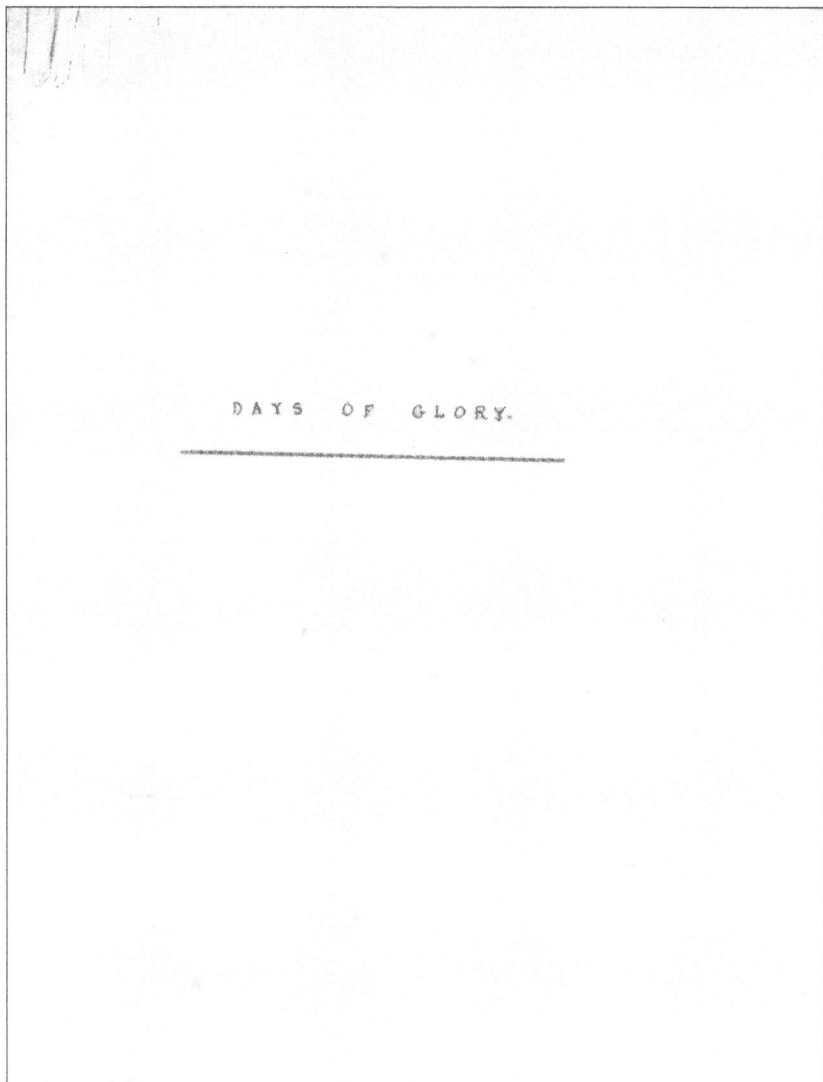

DAYS OF GLORY.

6. Title page of Part Two of FOREVER AND EVER, from Typescript A

7. Maximine Portaz, 14 June 1933, age 27. Her inscription on the back: "Glorious 1933."

Chapter 6

1933

(30th January)

---

*"Für was wir zu kämpfen haben, ist die
Sicherung des Bestehens und der Ver-
mehrung unserer Rasse und unseres Volkes,
die Ernährung seiner Kinder und Reinhal-
tung des Blutes, die Freiheit und Unabhäng-
igkeit des Vaterlandes, auf daß unser Volk
zur Erfüllung der auch ihm vom Schöpfer
des Universums zugewiesenen Mission
heranzureifen vermag."*

— Mein Kampf [1]

Then came the Day of days, the Day of joy and power, the
birthday of the reborn West; the Day when after thirteen
years of superhuman struggle Thou tookedst in Thy hand
the destiny of those whom Thou so lovedest — of those
whom all the Gods had willed; in our wondrous times, to
be the strongest and the best.

---

[1] *"We must fight to secure the existence and continuation of our race and
our people, the sustenance of our children and the purity of our blood, the
freedom and independence of the fatherland, so that our people may mature
in order to fulfill the mission assigned us by the creator of the universe"*
(*Mein Kampf*, p. 234, trans. R. G. Fowler; the original text is empha-
sized throughout).

There, like an ocean, stood the immense expectant crowd, restless and hopeful,—loving—but not yet daring to be sure; waiting to greet the long-awaited news; waiting to know that Thou hadst won; waiting to live the finest hour in the long life of struggling Germany,—the opening of the New Era, culmination of all the patient daily heroisms of recent years and of all those of yore. Minutes succeeded one another, and each one seemed an hour. Within thousands of breasts, hearts beat faster and faster as time went on. Every man held his breath. As the parched earth awaits the fecundating rain after the long ordeal of the arid season, in lands where rain-failure means death; as the world wrapped in gloom awaits the coming Dawn, so did Thy people on that day, gathered in growing thousands before the Presidential Palace of the Reich, await the magic words: the announcement of Thy triumph—and of theirs.

There was a movement in the crowd, and, for a second, utter silence. And in that solemn silence rose the voice of Thy close friend and faithful fighter of the early days, first in the Land after Thyself.[2] And the voice said: "Our Leader is in power!" For another second, there was silence,—a different silence; the silence of the thirsty earth communing with the heavens in the first drop of rain, as wind abates, the silence of unutterable joy verging on ecstasy. And then, out of the frenzied human ocean, one thunderous outcry burst forth all of a sudden, echoing the single voice and amplifying it a hundred thousandfold; one long-resounding elemental outcry, one endless roar of joy,—voice of Thy people; Voice of God Who within Nature's Chosen ones abideth,—: "Our Leader is in power! We are free!" And men shook hands with one another; and women threw themselves in one another's arms for joy; and tears of joy ran down their beaming faces.

Then, slowly did the enthusiastic crowd disperse in all directions, each man or woman, youth or maiden, carrying

---

[2] Hermann Göring

far and wide the glorious tidings of the Day: "Our Leader is now in power! Germany is risen!" And through the length and breadth of the yet mutilated Land, bells rang, and drums and martial trumpets resounded, and their music had not for centuries expressed such happiness. From every window broad flags hung, bearing the sacred Sign both of the Sun and of the Aryan Race. And along the crowded streets, under those endless rows of waving banners blood-red, black, and white, the now immortal Storm Troopers, whose constant sacrifice and bitter struggle had carried Thee to power, marched full of pride singing the immortal song.

And throughout every land recently torn away from Thy defeated Fatherland, and throughout every land in which Thy people lived, cut off from the main Realm by artificial frontiers, be it for centuries, an immense hope greeted the glorious tidings, by now broadcasted to the world: the hope that soon the brotherhood of blood would be the only link uniting all Thy people in one proud greater Reich; that soon under the impetus of Thy new living faith, all artificial boundaries would fall; that soon, in freedom, strength and joy, Thy people would expand towards the east, towards the west, in spite of other nations' jealous opposition, ful-filling the great destiny allotted them by Nature, whether in peace or in war.

❖ ❖ ❖

The age-old enemies of higher mankind were aghast; for in that loud outburst of frenzied joy that echoed from new Germany throughout the world, as well as in that immense silent hope that they could not suppress, they heard the death-knell of their long-established rule and felt the first signs of the end of their ascendancy — forever. They hated Thee and dreaded Thee. And in their secret councils, they started to prepare the satanic network of lies and of bar-gains by which they planned to stir against Thee and Thy people the stupid fury of the great unthinking human herd of every race and tongue, — of that dull universal herd that knew Thee not and could not feel the beauty of Thy dream.

A few among the better men of the wide world beyond Thy realm, welcomed Thy rising as the Dawn which they themselves awaited. And fewer still had been awaiting it as long and as consistently as I.

As one salutes from the seashore the Sun millions of miles away, so greeted I from afar the news of that tremendous Day; so welcomed I the announcement of Thy power; so did I worship Thee within my heart, my Leader, Giver of a new life to Thy great people,[3] Giver of a new pride and faith to every Aryan worthy of this race, now and forevermore!

And as the echo of Thy people's joy reached me, I thought of the stupendous dream that had been mine for ages: the dreams of real Aryan leadership throughout the world. Alone in our times couldst Thou make that great dream become a living fact. Alone a world under Thy rule could be that place of order and of beauty, that healthy Heathen world that I so long had craved[4] for. And in my heart I longed to see Thy conquering spirit smash all the man-made creeds of false equality. And in my heart I longed to see Thy conquering Greater Reich extend, one day, to every shore; the brotherhood of Aryan blood abolish man-made boundaries; and Thy inspired followers — the élite of the world — rule the whole earth, forevermore!

---

[3] The words "Giver of a new life to Thy great people" are omitted in Typescript B.

[4] Reading "craven" as "craved."

Chapter 7

1935

"... eine neue Weltanschauung und
nicht eine neue Wahlparole."

—*Mein Kampf* [1]

A beautiful medieval town, full of the joy and pageantry of our grand new era: old Nuremberg.[2] Houses with slanting roofs, crossed wooden beams and latticed windows, and flowerpots on every windowsill; and, hanging large and bright from these, thousands of blood-red flags bearing the holy Sign—the immemorial Swastika—in black in midst of a white disk; cathedrals in the gothic style, with sculptured spires reaching the sky, and statues of the Virgin-Mother and of bygone saints proclaiming the aspiration of the soul towards the Unattainable. And, marching past their doors and past those houses of another age, the Young Men of today singing triumphantly the song of pride and resurrection—blended in one: the old; the new; eternal Germany; eternal western Aryandom once more awake out of its Christian slumber. And in the immense Stadium near the town, under the eyes of half a million people, the *Reichsparteitag*, the ritual consecration of that miraculous awakening, in untold splendour, lasting days and nights.

---

[1] "... a new worldview, and not a new election slogan" (*Mein Kampf*, p. 243, trans. R. G. Fowler).

[2] Savitri consistently misspells "Nuremberg" (English)/"Nürnberg" (German) as "Nüremberg." I have used the English spelling throughout.

In the sunshine: the sacrament of Labour; the worship of the Earth in her fecundity, and of the strength and skill of Aryan Man, her fairest Child,[3] her pride, the brightest fruit of her delight in the Sun's long embrace; the sacrament of the creative skill of Aryan Man as corn-grower and miner and weapon-maker, and worker of the wonders of the lightning-power, in harmony with [the] ends of life and truth, in harmony with the great purpose of the Sun on earth—the rule in glory of the Sun-born Race.

With martial music, songs[,] and flags, bearing upon their shoulders the sacred Instruments of Labour—the Spade that opens Mother Earth to the life-giving Sun-rays—in came the proud young men, in squadrons of twice nine; behind them came the labour-Leaders, and the girls—the healthy working mothers of tomorrow, serene and strong as Mother Earth. And as parading soldiers present arms, so did these youths, in ceremonial gestures, present their spades, weapons of peaceful power. And loud and clear, between the martial songs evoking those who died for Germany during the liberation struggle; between two solemn tunes played on the throbbing drums, their young voices repeated the ritual formula: "Ready are we, indeed!"—ready to till the divine Land, the Fatherland, whose life is ours; ready to make it prosperous; ready to make it great!

And Thou spokest to them and to the many thousands, my beloved Leader—*our* Leader! And thousands of right arms outstretched in the sunshine greeted Thy words; and from[4] thousands of breasts came forth the rhythmic cry of frenzied pride and joy—and love—the cry of Thy new Germany: "*Sieg! Heil!*"

❖ ❖ ❖

---

[3] In Typescripts A and B, the word "Son" appears. In Typescript A, it is changed by hand to "Child."

[4] The words "thousands of right arms outstretched in the sunshine greeted Thy words; and from" are omitted in Typescript B.

In the dark night, the Sacrament of Silence—and Thy apotheosis, O my Leader, along with that of Germany, in the Temple of Light.[5]

In granite immobility, there stood the Brown Battalions, in thick formations between which stretched long straight empty spaces. A living picture of the conscious few, who, throughout endless Time, had kept Thy everlasting truth alive within their hearts, and watched, and hoped against all hope, and waited for the long-desired Aryan Dawn; they stood in heavy darkness awaiting Thee. With them, the thousands waited, in utter silence and without a ray of light upon their faces.

Then, suddenly, as Thou steppedest forth into the largest avenue that led to Thy exalted Seat, hundreds of blue transparent pillars—columns of dreamlike light—struck the dark sky from countless hidden sources all round the outer walls of the great Stadium, surrounding Thee as Thou walkedest on; surrounding Thy motionless Fighters, and all the silent, spellbound crowd; cutting off from the world the privileged enclosure—the consecrated space—where first among all Aryans of the West, Thy people were communing with their own proud soul, becoming conscious of the Godhead of their Race.

Thou reachedest Thy place above the crowd—above the broader outer world—and Thou stoodest in silence; the silence of five hundred thousand men standing together intently, in common faith, in common prayer, in common adoration of that One real God: their Nation's Soul; their Race's deeper soul;[6] the bright Soul of the Sun awake with-

---

[5] A handwritten note in Typescript A reads: "*Lichtdom* was actually the word used for this extraordinary sight." The *Lichtdom* or Cathedral of Light was created by focusing the beams of spotlights into the sky. Albert Speer remarked ironically that it proved to be his most enduring structure.

[6] The words "deeper soul" were omitted in Typescript B.

in themselves. In silence, utter silence didst Thou wait with
them—the silence of the grave before the stir of resurrec-
tion; the silence of primeval Night, mother of everything,
before the stir of Life.

Then slowly, from the limits of the Stadium—slowly and
silently—endless processions of flag-bearers poured in be-
tween the thick formations of the Brown Battalions. Under
the ghostly blue reflected light of that unearthly row of
phosphorescent columns that held the Stadium in a magic
circle, on they went; and on them, rested a ray of light. On
they went, bright red streams converging at Thy feet, slow-
ly and silently—streams of the new life-blood, irresistibly
quickening that immense body lying in the darkness in
deathlike immobility. And silence reigned; the magic si-
lence in which creative forces work irresistibly; the ecstatic
silence in which creative love communes with God, that is
to say, with everlasting Life. Silence, for half an hour, for an
hour, or more? And then, all of a sudden, like a creative
spell out of that radiant stillness,[7] the songs of life and
pride and conquest; and then, Thy speech, from that high
place,—from that first altar of the new Aryan Faith;—Thy
speech to Germany in adoration before Thee, and, beyond
Germany, to me, six thousand miles away, to whom the
waves of aether carried it; to the whole Aryan Race. And
then, those songs again: the Song of the dead hero, Horst
Wessel, now alive, forever and ever, and the well-known
national anthem: "Germany above all . . ."

"Above all?" did then many ask within their hearts, already
with suspicion and hidden jealousy. And the songs and Thy
people's cheers, and Thy voice and Thy silence, and theirs,
all echoed: "Yes!" And I, remembering the centuries by-
gone, and that long fruitless, hopeless struggle of Aryan
man against the Jewish yoke[8] from the day Paul of Tarsus

---

[7] "Silence" in Typescript A is replaced with "stillness" in Type-
script B.

[8] Reading "joke" in both Typescripts as "yoke."

had set[9] foot in Athens, thought: "Why not? Yes, why not, my Leader's countrymen, if ye be worthy of Him and worthy of your task? If ye can lead us all to freedom and to glory, as He leads You?"

❖ ❖ ❖

In the sunshine, the Sacrament of Consecration of the flags. Thou heldest in Thy hand the "Flag of Blood," the one that the Sixteen first Martyrs bore, when, in their vain attempt to carry Thee to power, they fell; for Germany and Thee, twelve years before. And in Thy other hand, Thou heldest the new flags—the ones that were to inspire Thy many younger Fighters with the burning faith of the old; the ones that were to carry forth, along the highways, south and north, and east and west, to all Germanic people still outside the Reich, Thy great message of unity and pride and strength within their folds.

Through Thee, the Leader and the Saviour, through Thee, the living Reich,—the priest of the National Soul, that very Soul itself,—ran the mysterious power of the dead; the magic power of boundless love and pure blood[,] shed for love's sake without regret; the magic power of blood on which all greatness lies. It ran into the bright-red folds of the new flags, into the[10] snow-white disk and the age-old Sign of Power which in the disk they bore: the holy Swastika, Sign of the Life force in the Sun among the ancient Aryans, Sign of the new Awakening of Germany and of the Aryan Race, Thy Sign, our Sign, forevermore.

And it gave them the virtue of the "Flag of Blood"; the virtue of the dead who fell for Germany to live in freedom and honour;[11] the virtue of the dead who fell for Thee to rule, and for Thy people to become, in Europe and Beyond the

[9] In Typescript B, "his" is omitted after "set."
[10] The words "into the" are omitted in Typescript B.
[11] The words "the virtue of the dead who fell for Germany to live in freedom and honour" are omitted in Typescript B.

narrow boundaries of Europe, the herald of Awakening Aryandom.

I was not there. From far away, I watched the new stupendous rites: the first rites of the new civilization that I had craved[12] for, age after age, since the decay of Aryan man.

I was not there — alas! And yet I felt that the Day of my dream had come, at last; that the old pride of the Sun-born had won against the lying teachings which[13] Aryan man had once acclaimed, to his disgrace; that my own cult of health and strength and youthful manly beauty, my double aspiration at the same time Nordic and Grecian, my ever-living Soul, silenced and mocked for fifteen hundred years, had won, through Thee and through Thy Nation.

I watched Thee transfer to the age-old Symbol of our Race, that marked Thy flags, the fluid of rejuvenation, the magic virtue of the modern heroes' blood. And in my heart, I hailed the blessed colours, and thought: "May I see Thee wave over East and West, Sign of the domination of the Sun-born, eternal Swastika, Sign of the Best!"

---

[12] Reading "craven" as "craved."
[13] "That" in both Typescripts is hand-corrected to "which" in Typescript A.

Chapter 8

1938

"Würde man die Menschheit in drei
Arten einteilen: in Kulturbegründer, Kul-
turträger und Kulturzerstörer, dann
käme als Vertreter der ersten wohl nur
der Arier in Frage."
— *Mein Kampf* [1]

And years rolled on. And Thy astounding power extended un-
disputed over the ever-greater Reich. And the wide world, —
the world of the deluded, — experienced increasing awe at the
sight of Thy greatness. — And I adored Thee all the more.

From many thousand miles away, where Fate had willed that I
should stay, I spoke according to Thy spirit in the name of
truth everlasting. Alone, I walked along Thy way, never forget-
ting that, one day, I would return, and see Thee in Thy glory;
that, one day, to me among all, the untold privilege would fall,
in the language of future times, to tell the Aryans of all climes,
the unsuspected meaning of Thy story.

I travelled and I spoke. From halls in Indian towns, from shady
places under banyan trees throughout the Indian countryside, I

---

[1] "Were we to divide mankind into three kinds: culture founders,
culture bearers, and culture destroyers, then probably only the Aryan
could be considered as representative of the first" (*Mein Kampf*, p. 243,
trans. R. G. Fowler).

stirred, in countless dusky black-eyed crowds,[2] both age-old loyalty to Aryan Gods and hatred of the modern yoke of money,—and in an Aryan minority, our common racial pride. I spoke of the twilight of Western Heathendom and of the early days of the dark era in which the Jewish creed of Man prevailed at last against the Aryan creeds of life. And I quoted the bitter words in which Emperor Julian, dying upon the battlefield, is said to have expressed the despair of his heart at the sight of that world that he had tried in vain to rescue from decay: "O Galilean, thou hast won!" I exalted eastern Aryandom, silent, but still alive in old caste-ridden India—faithful in its expectant immobility. I fought, with all the fire of my heart, the levelling creeds of *Man*,—the Jewish creeds, whatever the garb in which they might be clad. And I spoke of Thy glorious Dawn, and of the coming days in which the racial aristocracy of East and West would stand together and together[3] hail the divine truth preserved in immemorial Aryan Writ. And many times I quoted Thee, Soul of the new world-wide Awakening; Son and Avenger of the Aryan Gods both Germanic and Grecian, Saviour who hast answered at last, the sixteen hundred year old call of him who failed.

In the tropical atmosphere rang Thy eternal words, Thy words of truth and pride, expressed by me in a different tongue. And many dusky faces would brighten and many people clap their hands, for in those words the crowd could recognize the Wisdom that had governed India in immemorial bygone days. And many a fairer face among the crowd—a face with noble features and with thoughtful eyes—would look intently up to me, for in those words the few would hear and feel the echo of that Aryan Wisdom that their forefathers from the glorious distant North had brought with them to be the wisdom of all lands. And once an old man came to me when I had finished speaking, and said, alluding to Thy words: "From which most hallowed Writ of Ancient days have you quoted this truth?"

---

[2] In Typescript B, "crowds" is replaced by "people."
[3] In Typescript B, "and together" is omitted.

And tears came to my eyes as I measured the bridge that Thou hast thrown over the stream of Time between our world and its remotest youth, between Thy beloved people and the fair warriors of their race—of our common race—by whom the Aryan fame filled India so long ago; over the immensity of space, between Thy beloved Land and any land where lives and rules the spirit of the Aryan race. I suddenly remembered that I stood on the very border of the Aryan world—hardly a hundred miles away from Burma and from China. And my heart leaped within my breast as I uttered Thy name.

. . .

8. Savitri Devi's husband Asit Krishna Mukherji (1904-1977), March 1962

And then, I met the wisest of the southern Aryans, the silent Friend who understood the meaning of Thy[4] Dawn, and who, through written word and thought, and patient action in the dark, was planning and preparing the staggering extension of

---

[4] In Typescript B, "Thy" is omitted.

Thy grand New Order to all the world.[5]

And the Wise One told me: "Go back, where duty calls you! Go back, the time has come; go straight to Him who is the Leader of the West, for He alone your burning faith will fathom, for He alone your love and hate will welcome and give you all the means to do your best. Don't remain here; go straight to Him, who is Life and Resurrection; to unsuspected fields of joyous action without regret and without rest!"

"In a year's time or a little more, when I have done all that I can do here; when, in immense Aryavarta, more people understand why I have come, and are ready to hail our spreading light, then I shall go—and tell my brothers: 'See! Through Eastern ways, with Eastern words, and with that understanding which freedom from all ties save yours has given me, I have hastened the fulfilment of the age-old dream of Aryan domination; of *your* great dream of world-wide might!'"

But the wise One replied: "Go *now!*—for it will be too late in a year's time!"

Why did I not believe him? Conscious of Thy great heathen Dawn, why did I stay so far away from danger and from duty? What made me blinded to all the signs of the threatening storm? In spite of all my love and hate, what held me back? An evil fate—or glorious plans of which no man could know? Plans of the Gods almighty?

---

[5] Savitri refers to A. K. Mukherji as the "Wise One" throughout.

Chapter 9

1940

"... und da, als der Tod gerade geschäftig hineingriff in unsere Reihen, da erreichte das Lied auch uns, und wir gaben es nun wieder weiter: Deutschland, Deutschland über alles, über alles in der Welt!"

— *Mein Kampf* [1]

Which one of us does not, today, with tears, remember that great year among all years: glorious 1940? Which one of us does not today with bitterness look back to those staggering days, in which the noise and flames and smoke of spreading war answered on Thy behalf the world's unjust attack?

O great One, Leader of the Best, from Thy young Reich, towards the East, towards the West, towards the hallowed North, on land and sea and in the skies, in irresistible formations, Thy men of iron poured forth, for Thee, for greater Germany and all that Germany implies. The song of freedom, pride and power accompanied their onward march across the boundaries of seven nations. And there was nothing that could halt their godlike thrust . . . And from its northernmost promontory facing

---

[1] "... and then, as Death busily reached straight into our ranks, the song also reached us, and we took it up and passed it on: 'Germany, Germany over everything, over everything in the world!'" (*Mein Kampf*, p. 181, trans. R. G. Fowler).

the Pole, down to the smiling shores of the great Inner Sea, the continent that had believed the Jewish[2] lies, — the continent that had rejected Thee — lay at Thy feet within the dust!

Unforgettable days and nights of permanent elation, when every blessed hour brought me through subtle aether-waves, along with Thy beloved voice, the joy of further victory! When both the sunlit earth, so bright in its tropical glory, and all the countless lights of starry space seemed to tell me: "Rejoice! The Western Resurrection that you have waited for so long has come at last; and He, the Saviour Whom you loved unknowingly for centuries, and Whom you hailed but yesterday as Leader of his people and of all those who recognise and who welcome his people's place in history, now rules the Aryan race according to your dream!"

From the other end of the earth, I watched the fire of war spread.

The sky was blue; the Sun was hot; the joy and pride of conquest made my face beam. Stronger and stronger in my heart grew the sweet certitude of Thy invincibility. One day, — I knew not when, but, surely, thought I, "soon" — I would go back and see all Europe under Thee . . . It mattered little, then, whether I were or not, for the time being[,] on the spot.

I pictured in my mind Thy endless rows of armoured tanks, rushing through woods and moors and through deserted towns along the international highways; through mud and sand, along the river banks. I pictured in my mind Thy fleeing enemies under the pouring rain — the roaring sea before them, the angry sky above them, the dark night all around them, Thy battalions behind them — nearer and nearer every second — and in their hearts, more powerful than all, the overwhelming terror of Thy name![3] I pictured in my mind the famous Arch of Triumph; the

---

[2] Capitalizing "jewish" in keeping with Savitri's general practice.
[3] Referring to the evacuation of fleeing British and French troops at Dunkirk from 26 May to 4 June 1940.

no less famous Avenue, pride of the conquered Capital; and under it, and along it, the unforgettable Parade!⁴

9. Savitri Devi's 1940 Passport Photo

There stood and marched those who, in Ypres and elsewhere, had fought alongside Thee during the First World War; those who, within the grip of death, had sung along with Thee, the conquering Hymn of love in which echoed the call of joyful Duty: "Germany, Germany above all . . . !" There stood and

---

⁴ Referring to the German army's entry into Paris on 14 June 1940, during which they marched down the avenue des Champs-Élysées beneath the Arc de Triomphe. This was expressly not presented as a victory parade (*Siegesparade*), in order to spare the patriotic feelings of the French, but merely an "unofficial march" (*inoffizielier Vorbeimarsch*), a distinction largely ignored then and now.

marched also, like unto living Nordic gods, Thy fair and strong Young men, hope of the resurrected Reich, hope of the Western world, messengers of everlasting Aryan faith.

Moving in incredible order, there they were, the ones I had been longing for ever since the decay of Aryandom — over two thousand years; the ones I had been seeking in the immortal forms of bygone Grecian gods, and the immortal characters of Aryan heroes held as gods in India to this day: the real earthly "shining ones": my better brothers and Thy sons!

And as they went the music played, and as they went they sang the new hymn of the Strong and Free, — the Song of the young Hero, who, ten years before, had died for Thee: "Along all highways, very soon, will our banners flutter; slavery is to last only a short time more!"[5] And there indeed, the holy blood-red Flags, bearing within their midst in black on white the eternal Swastika, fluttered triumphantly above the glittering helmets, above the cadenced March, above the conquered Continent, in the warm air of June.

❖ ❖ ❖

From the Eastern world far away, where I then stood, a cry had sprung — a cry of admiration, for Thee, for those who followed Thee; for Thy young resurrected nation.

One day, a dusky youth of the Far South greeted me with amazing words, as though the Gods had chosen to express their unshakable wisdom through his mouth. "Fair Lady, believe me," he said, "I too within my heart adore your Leader, now Lord of the West! — For He has come to overthrow the Money-power in the world; for He has come in order to set up the wisdom of the Shining Ones Who conquered us in bygone days — the Aryan Wisdom of all times; the Wisdom of the Best — against the Christian way of Life; in order to fulfil the words of the most holy Writ: 'Age after age, I come . . .'; for He

---

[5] "Die Fahne hoch" by Horst Wessel.

is God in human garb, the One Who never fails."[6]

Another day, a fair-skinned man in orange-coloured robes—a man, of those who look beyond the Realm of Time—sat by my side and told me: "Your Continent has now within its midst another Incarnation of the great World-Sustaining-One. No longer weep over its long decay! But follow Him, and you shall win, in the long run. The struggle of today is but another phase of the perennial Struggle. And He is Light and Life come down to earth again to lead the Aryan World once more along the glorious Way!"[7]

And in the glaring homage of the village youth, echo of popular insight, as well as in that of the serene ascetic, I heard the world proclaim in space and time, that Thou wast right, and foreign men on foreign shores, age after age, in speeches yet unknown, exalt Thy wisdom and Thy might.

And I was happy, even though so far away. And I too sang the conquering Song, with my right arm outstretched, while the Wise One, the truest of our true Allies, now bound to me through solemn mystic ties,[8] stood by my side and smiled, as though his eyes could see, beyond six thousand miles of land and sea, the Parade of Thy trusted Bodyguard along the conquered Avenue, the rush of Thy glittering planes across the sky.

❖ ❖ ❖

---

[6] The young man was named Khudiram, and Savitri relates his story in her essay "Hitlerism and the Hindu World," *The National Socialist*, no. 2 (Fall 1980): 18–20. It is available online under its original title, "Hitlerism and Hindudom" at the Savitri Devi Archive, www.savitridevi.org.

[7] Probably Swami Satyananda, the leader of the Hindu Mission in Calcutta, who seems to have been the first to suggest to Savitri that Adolf Hitler was an avatar of the Hindu god Vishnu, the sustainer of order. See *And Time Rolls On*, 24, 119.

[8] Savitri Devi and A. K. Mukherji were married in Calcutta in a civil ceremony on 29 September 1939 and in a religious ceremony on 9 June 1940.

Oh, great days! We were all so happy, then! Before our eyes, we saw the map of the expanding Reich unfold itself in all directions; and all our dreams materialise! In the glory of our reborn heathen civilisation, ahead of us, we saw, a future of world domination, that was never to fail . . .

Oh, great days! Whether on the spot or far away, we greeted with the Sunrise, Thy daily triumphs upon land and sea;[9] we watched the Gods come down from heaven at Thy call, and fight for Thee. We were so happy, then! — And I, the happiest of all!

10. Savitri Devi with Japanese family, November 1939, probably in Calcutta

---

[9] The words "we greeted with the Sunrise, Thy daily triumphs upon land and sea" were omitted from Typescript B.

Chapter 10

1942

"Nun weiß der Jude zu genau, daß er in
seiner tausendjährigen Anpassung wohl
europäische Völker zu unterhöhlen und
zu geschlechtslosen Bastarden zu erzieh-
en vermag, allein einem asiatischen Na-
tionalstaat von der Art Japans dieses
Schicksal kaum zuzufügen in der Lage
wäre. . . . Er scheut in seinem tausendjäh-
rigen Judenreich einen japanischen Na-
tionalstaat und wünscht deshalb dessen
Vernichtung noch vor Begründung
seiner eigenen Diktatur. So hetzt er heute
die Völker gegen Japan wie einst gegen
Deutschland . . . ."

— *Mein Kampf* [1]

To the furthermost Isles of Dawn, the struggle now extended . . .

---

[1] "Now the Jew knows all too well that he, with his thousand-year
adaptation, is probably able to undermine European peoples and turn
them into raceless bastards, but in an Asiatic national state like Japan
he is hardly in the position to promote this fate. . . . In his thousand-
year Jewish *Reich* he dreads a Japanese national state and thus wishes
it annihilated even before founding his own dictatorship. So today he
incites the nations to hate Japan as he once did against Germany"
(*Mein Kampf*, pp. 723–24, trans. R. G. Fowler).

More and more irresistible, the war-cry of those distant Isles had burst forth at the Gods' command, and within space invisible, over a stretch of fifteen thousand miles of hostile land, with that of our martial Song, its echo had blended.

These were also great days,—days of expanding power, in which, as though on their way to a feast, Thy yet unvanquished armies marched, full of self-confidence and joy, across the Russian plains, further and further east; while further still one could admire a world ridding itself of foreign chains at Japan's call, amidst the Pacific on fire.

Across the Russian plains, from North to South, from West to East, as though they were going forth to meet and greet the Rising Sun, on went Thy inspired Armies, that seemed invincible; Thy Special Storm formations,[2] spreading along their way, through lands that seemed unreachable, the fear of Thee into the hearts of newly conquered nations, further and further every day, and rounding up, as they advanced, and sending to their doom—their proper place—the arch-enemies of the Aryan race![3]

From faraway Japan, through conquered Indo-China, through the Isles of the Southern Seas, and the thick jungles of Malay and those of Burma, from East to West, from South to North, our bravest allies poured forth, suddenly like a swarm of bees. Since that great night on which the world had seen, amazed, amidst the thunder of exploding bombs, in lurid light, a hundred burning ships trying to flee from Pearl Harbor ablaze,[4] one place after the other had surrendered to those who in the Pacific now fought for Thee.

Hong Kong; Manila, Saigon, Surabaya, Penang, and soon Kuala Lumpur were in their hands; and every dawning day brought news of further conquests, until, exactly 2602 years after the

---

[2] The S.S. or the *Einsatzgruppen*.
[3] The Jews.
[4] On 7 December 1941.

Empire of the Rising Sun is said to have been founded, burst forth, to the four corners of the world astounded, the most staggering news of all: that of the fall of Singapore.[5]

With that stronghold, which had, so long, seemed inexpugnable, it was as though our enemies had lost the bastion of their might. Joy unutterable, and frenzied hopes and dreams of domination filled out hearts and made our countenances bright. And while the Wise One who, in patient secrecy, had made it possible for Thy Allies to win their way through Burma, quietly smoked his water pipe, I paced the marble floor in proud elation, and sang the Song of war, like on the Day the vanguard of thy hosts had entered conquered Paris, — like on Pearl Harbor Night.

❖ ❖ ❖

Great days indeed were these! Before the lightning thrust of Thy gallant allies, the enemies of Thy New Order fled in terror, along the dusty roads and through the swamps, while behind them filling the bright-red sky, slowly unfurled itself in thick black coils the smoke of hundreds of burning oil tanks; or else, hard-pressed on every side, they rushed here and there in dismay, seeking in vain, within the jungles all ablaze, a miraculous way by which to flee and hide; two mighty hunters[6] led the chase: the fire that crawled and ran and roared under the trees, and, calmly awaiting them outside, ready to shoot them dead as they came out, our efficient friends the Japanese.

Soon fell Rangoon and Mandalay . . . The gallant warriors of Dawn steadily pushed on and on, up the great Irrawady Valley and beyond; though plains and hills and forests, without rest, nearer Bengal, nearer Assam, nearer Upper Hindustan, where East meets West, a few miles further every day. And through a solid chain of trusted men, the Wise One sent them messages,

---

[5] On 15 February 1942.

[6] Probably a reference to two Japanese commanders, whose identity can only be guessed.

so that more of Thy enemies might perish at their hands. And we waited to welcome them as they would reach Calcutta, and past our house march forth on the way west, on their way north, to further lands.

Oh, it was sweet to watch them come! And it was sweet to know that, through our humble agency, more thousands of Thy foes—more servants of the world-wide Money-power, traitors to their own race; more men of those who were now pouring fire upon Thy beloved people—would perish in their turn within the flames, in Burma's jungles far away, or be sent off to toil for Thy allies, no one knew where on Asian soil! And it was sweet to see the impact of Thy armies break all resistance within mighty Russia, and thy Young Men march on and on and on, towards the Caucasus, towards the Volga, towards the endless Lands of Dawn!

❖ ❖ ❖

We all thought Stalingrad would fall; and we all thought Calcutta would soon be in Thy Allies' hands. As warm sunbeams fill golden space, and then suddenly vanish, before the growing darkness of the storm, so then stupendous dreams,[7] were to leave no trace but that of bitter disillusion within our hearts, carried us right beyond the realm of dire reality; for then we felt, for then we thought, in all sincerity, that we had won . . .

By the Wise One I sat, picturing in my mind the endless eastward thrust of Thy victorious legions, for the Greater Reich and for Thee, from the shores of the Caspian Sea, past Bukhara and Samarkand, and through restless Afghanistan—through unknown regions—down to the heart of Hindustan. I pictured them along the old Conqueror's Road; the road[8] that Alexander took when Fate had willed him to bring war to meditative India; the road the ancient Aryans followed four thousand years

---

[7] The words "before the growing darkness of the storm, so then stupendous dreams" were omitted from Typescript B.

[8] The words "the road" were omitted from Typescript B.

before. I pictured them, as though their coming were a certitude. I pictured them along the Kabul Valley, and then within that haunted solitude of brick-red rocks and bright-blue sky, full of hallucinating beauty, that leads to Jamrud and Peshawar. I pictured them,—the same ones who had stood in the great Party Rallies—glad the command of duty had sent them there, singing along their way the well-known song: "We shall march further on, even if all should fall to pieces; for Germany belongs to us today, and tomorrow . . . the whole world!" The mighty rocks sent back the spell-like words and the vibrations of the horns of brass mingled their grandeur with the grandeur of the site. And in the dry, transparent air, the red and brown hills seemed more bright, with their chaotic outlines and dark shadows. And in the sunshine fluttered the proud Swastika flag, red, black and white. And on they went, Thy soldiers,— my brothers bold and fair—like their forerunners of Antiquity, through the historic Khyber Pass!

They would indeed "march further on," and reach imperial Delhi; and there Thy brave Allies would meet . . . And war would end, and I would see both Lands of Dawn and Lands of Sunset at Thy feet;—redeemed and free. And between the Far East, extended realm of the Sons of the Rising Sun and Thy extended Realm, the Aryan West, the Wise One, hidden worker of great deeds, and of all Thy allies the best, would rule the South, from Ceylon to the Russian border, in faith and truth, according to the needs of Thy new Order. And under him in spirit no less than in name broad Hindustan would become Aryavarta again![9]

And I would stand by Thee in happiness and glory, I, the Link between East and West and between North and South; the eternal Aryan Soul in woman's earthly garb; and in the famous

---

[9] This sentence is a composite of sentences from Typescript A "And under him broad Hindustan again, in spirit no less than in name, Aryavarta would!" and Typescript B "And under him in spirit no less than in name broad Hindustan would rebecome again!"

marble hall in which has stood the Peacock Throne,[10] in the
name of strange multitudes unknown to Thee and to Thy peo-
ple, my eyes and heart fixed upon Thee alone, hail thee as
Leader of the reborn world! — my Leader!

❖ ❖ ❖

Oh, why did that great dream not become true? Why did a hos-
tile Fate suddenly change the course of things, and, kindling
treachery on every front abroad, while letting loose the hell of
hate over Thy Fatherland in streams of fire, set out to break
Thy eagle's wings? Why was it so that before they could reach
to mastery over the Sunset Lands, Thy beloved people fair and
bold were first to hold the palm of martyrdom within their
hands?

11. Savitri Devi with unidentified Japanese lady, 1943, probably in Calcutta

---

[10] At the Red Fort in Delhi, the seat of the Mughal Emperors.

Part Three
DAYS OF HORROR

12. Title page of Part Three of FOREVER AND EVER, from Typescript A

13. Savitri Devi, July 1945, probably in Calcutta

Chapter 11

1945

"Was folgte, waren entsetzliche Tage
und noch bösere Nächte—ich wußte, daß
alles verloren war. Auf die Gnade des
Feindes zu hoffen, konnten höchstens
Narren fertigbringen oder—Lügner und
Verbrecher. In diesen Nächten wuchs
mir der Haß, der Haß gegen die Urheber
dieser Tat."

—*Mein Kampf* [1]

"PROSE" VERSION FROM
TYPESCRIPTS A & B

Three more years of desperate struggle against the forces of disintegration; against the unseen Money-Power; its growing armament and all its lies; three more long years in which the Jew's allies sought in vain to destroy Thy Nation in endless streams of phosphorous and fire; three more long years in which, before the eyes of the bewildered world, Thy people stood the test, and in the midst of smoking ruins, fought the

---

[1] "What followed were horrible days and even worse nights—I knew that all was lost. To hope for the mercy of the enemy, only complete fools could bring that to pass—or liars and criminals. And in these nights, hatred grew in me, hatred of the authors of this deed" (*Mein Kampf*, pp. 225, trans. R. G. Fowler).

East and fought the West, as only gods could fight, and would
have won in spite of all—who knows?—had not increasing
treachery given new weapons to Thy foes!

But then,—after those months and months of untold sacrifice—
our darkest hour: surrender, with the trail of misery and bitter-
ness that it implies; the desecration of Thy Eagle's Nest by Jews
and slaves of Jews; and proud Germany torn in four between
her persecutors; and Thou—visible Soul of everlasting Germa-
ny, the Founder and Head of our new Faith of health and
pride—with Thy whole life's creation, dead—so the news said!

Oh, who will ever, now or in the future, tell the tale of hatred
and of rage of those atrocious days? The tale of mad despair[,]
of our passage into hell? The tale of the last ones who fell in
Libya's burning sands, or on the parched and shattered earth of
their own Fatherland, or in the snow and frost of the Russias'
Grim, white plains, on every battlefield, in loving faith, thy ho-
ly name upon their lips—up to the end—for honour to be safe,
while they knew all the rest was lost? The tale of the survivors,
of the survivors of the titanic fight, driven into captivity for
knowing Thou wast right? The tale of Thy uprooted people of
all the eastern parts of the great Reich, fleeing before the Rus-
sian hosts in the cold night only to meet, wherever they would
go, the sight of more invaders—more agents of the Jewish
might and self-ordained crusaders against our creed of Life
and Light? The tale of Thy whole Nation under the horrid four-
fold Occupation, which then barely began and was to last no
one yet knew how long?

❖ ❖ ❖

Oh, to sleep—to forget; and never to awake; never again to
know that once upon a time a wretched world existed in which
out of the slime of mediocre, dull humanity, a godlike Nation
had arisen, at the call of a godlike Man, believing in her own
invincibility, and lived and toiled and sang, in youthful joy and
glory, six great years long[,] and then, the stupid fury of that
mean and jealous world, for another six years resisted? Oh, to

sleep — to forget; never again to know, that under Thy New Order, firmly set in for centuries, all could have been so beautiful, but that, forevermore, because in spite of a series of Victories, we lost this war, it would hopelessly be just as before Thy dawning power — and worse, far worse; that this would be a God-forsaken world, full of our persecutors' fame; a world in which, henceforth, men would be taught to hate Thy people and to curse Thy name! A world[2] in which the very children of Thy trusted ones, now full of bitterness like I, would slowly have to learn to love Thy enemies or learn to lie! Or to sleep — to forget; to die! Of this tragic collapse of Thy splendid great Reich, not to know a thing anymore!

Thus thought I as I wandered, all alone, from place to place as far from crowded cities as it was possible, in order not to hear or read the news, in order not to know when the dark day I dreaded — the last day of the hallowed Reich — would be. Beyond the forms and colours of all things visible, two inner nightmares haunted me: the vision of Thee in the midst of Germany in ruins, and that of my own wasted life away from Thee.

Why had I not been all these long years at Thy side? For Thee and for the truth I had loved all my life, why was I not there now to fight — and die — with the two Words of faith and pride upon my lips, as thousands of my brothers? I who had always seen in Thee the Child of Light; I who from miles and miles away had cheered Thy growing might, but never seen Thy glory, now pictured to myself, with tears, Thy tragic Face against the background of the crumbling Reich. And like the deep thrust of a knife into my heart, the maddening thought come back, ever and ever more: in this hour of agony when all was lost, oh, why was I not there, to fight, to die, with the Reich's last defenders, for all that I adored?[3]

---

[2] In Typescript B, "a world" is added by hand.

[3] In this paragraph and the following one, I have followed the punctuation of Typescript B, which simplifies in a systematic — and thus probably deliberate fashion — the punctuation of Typescript A.

Oh, to sleep, to forget, now I could do no more! While in the distant West, events would take their course, in definitive noth- ingness, to lie, — to rest — freed from the nightmare of surren- der, freed from the nightmare of remorse for not having laid down my life in action at Thy side, in absolute unconsciousness forever to abide!

Thus thought I as, alone, in mountain fastnesses, or on the beaches, I would roam and roam. Facing me with noise and foam, the waterfalls and torrents, and facing me, the swelling Ocean tide, all seemed to say: "Come! Just a step into the depth, and you will be forever free; away from the haunting sight and thought of all your comrades' plight; away from the knowledge of the breakdown of their Nation, exalted home of all you love; away, away from the torment and horror of this hopeless world: you need, indeed, only to take a step into the roaring depth, in order to sleep — to forget!"

❖ ❖ ❖

And yet that step I did not take. For stronger even than despair within my bleeding heart was hate — hate of those who had brought about that awful fate upon Thy beloved[4] Nation. And stronger than the horror of the long nightmare was one of great aspiration: the will to live for sweet revenge's sake.

The will to live, in order that, one day, even if I never should see the resurrection of Thy great Reich in all its might, I should at least admire the coming scenes of the tremendous Play of Action and Reaction — heavenly Nemesis, tardy but unavoidable; — in order [that] I should see our persecutors fight among them- selves, and set each other's towns on fire; and that, remembering the untold suffering and the dismay their planes had once brought Germany night after night, I should then rejoice at the sight! The will to live,[5] in order that, even if I never should know

---

[4] Reading "loved" in both Typescripts as "beloved."

[5] "The will to live," is omitted in Typescript B.

the joy of Thy return,[6] I should at least watch *them* — the everlasting foes of Aryan man, the real[7] Killers of Thy people; and[8] those who now stood on their side, against Thee, against us — weep in their turn, and writhe, and burn, and die to my delight!

Yes, I would live, decided I, though life could only be one long torment for me; I would renounce the blessed peace of endless sleep and of forgetfulness, suffer the horror of defeat and all the hopelessness of a world henceforth ruled by those who hated Thee — suffer it all, be it for years, only wait and see that world in terror reap, in the long run, the fruits of its alliance with Thy foes.

In the meantime, the long-drawn nightmare had begun.

14. Savitri Devi, 1945, Calcutta
Her inscription on the back: "Not fair, not fat, but nearly forty."

---

[6] The phrase ", even if I never should know the joy of Thy return," is omitted in Typescript B.

[7] Typescript A reads "Thy foes, the killers of Thy people." In Typescript B, "Thy foes" is crossed out and "the everlasting foes of Aryan man, the real" is inserted by hand.

[8] In both Typescripts, the word "all" appears here, but in Typescript B, it is crossed out by hand.

"Verse" Variants

From Savitri's letter to George Lincoln Rockwell, 28 August 1965:

On the coast, at Varkala, at the foot of the ochre red rocks over which one could see palm woods, I looked at the Indian Ocean. I listened to it roar. I admired the strength of the enormous waves that came splashing up against the red rocks, or unfurling on the yellowish gray sand. Many years later—in one of my yet unpublished prose poems, *Forever and Ever*, I described my feelings of that day:

Oh, to sleep, to forget, to die! . . .
While in the distant West
events would take their course,
freed from the nightmare of surrender,
freed from the nightmare of remorse,
for not having laid down my life, in action at Thy side,
in absolute unconsciousness,
for ever to abide![9]

And I walked in to the sea:

Only another step,
into the roaring depth,
in order to sleep,
to forget!

I intended not to walk back. But as I had water up to my shoulders, or nearly, a thought went through my mind like lightning: *live* — . . .

---

[9] Savitri quotes exactly the same words in her letter to Rockwell of 4 January 1961.

Chapter 12

1946

"Wahrlich, auch diese Helden verdienten
einen Stein: 'Wanderer, der du nach
Deutschland kommst, melde der Heimat,
daß wir hier liegen, treu dem Vaterlande
und gehorsam der Pflicht.'"

—*Mein Kampf*[1]

In the dull sky, above the greenish sea, out of the mist, ap-
peared a great red Disk. And with their mighty wings wide-
open to resist the bitter blowing wind, the screaming gulls
passed by. And there stood I, upon the upper deck. As far as I
could see: the rolling waves under the rising Sun, bright-red
and without rays. All I could hear: the howl of the cold wind;
the seagulls' dismal cry. And there stood I upon the sea, near-
ing the coast of Europe after days of voyage—after years of ab-
sence—and thinking of the horror of existence among the fools

---

[1] "Truly, these heroes deserved a monument: 'Wanderer, you who
come to Germany, tell your homeland that here we lie, true to the
fatherland and obedient to duty'" (*Mein Kampf*, p. 224, trans. R. G.
Fowler). Hitler is paraphrasing Friedrich Schiller's words about the
death of Leonidas and the 300 Spartans at Thermopylae: "Wanderer,
kommst du nach Sparta, verkündige dorten, du habest/Uns hier
liegen gesehen, wie das Gesetz es befahl" ("Wanderer, if you go to
Sparta, proclaim there that you saw us lying here as the law com-
manded").

and criminals who hated Thee.[2]

Less than a thousand miles away from where the steamer sailed, I knew Thy Fatherland now lay under the victors' heel—a stretch of devastated continent; I knew the millions who had hailed Thy holy name all through these years, now walked in silence and hunger along the Way of blood and tears. And indignation, hate and anger grew at that thought within my heart. For though I could imagine the great inexorable Wheel of Destiny, slowly and steadily rolling on and avenging us, one day, I knew the blessed hour was yet too far away for me to feel it coming. And I wept. But as I saw the Disk so gorgeous in the midst of wind and fog, above the sea, "The everlasting Sun," thought I, "has never failed!" And so, while all lies Waste at our persecutors' feet, the everlasting Truth Thou hast proclaimed remains and shines, although ignored, unaltered above ruin and defeat. And in my heart once more I worshipped Thee.

Darker and darker grew the mist; dimmer and dimmer grew the sight of railway road and countryside, of suburbs and of city. And night succeeded day. So near and yet so far away, again the blood-red Disk hung in the dull grey sky. And day succeeded night.

The story of my brothers' humiliation, presented as a talk of victory, was shouted out to me unceasingly, from private and from public places, from morn to sunset and from then to morn, along with nauseating sermons about "right," freedom and human dignity, and our "re-education," so that a "better world" could dawn for all men of all races . . . and evil, Jewish-

---

[2] Savitri actually returned to Europe in November 1945, embarking on 2 November 1945 from Bombay and disembarking on 15 November in Southampton, where she took the boat train to London. Savitri relates other events from her return-voyage to Europe in "Heliodora's Homeward Journey," chapter 6 of *Long-Whiskers and the Two-Legged Goddess, or the true story of a "most objectionable Nazi" and . . . half-a-dozen cats* (Calcutta: Savitri Devi Mukherji, 1965).

looking faces would grin at me while they insulted Thee. And thus the long nightmare dragged on . . . and on.

The long nightmare . . . ; the vision of the ruins of Thy new Reich that was to us the one inspiring Force of Western Aryandom; its only living Soul; the vision of our foes now able to enforce their lying "liberty" upon the world, from pole to pole; of our foes, complacent tools within the hand of the almighty Jew, gloating over the charred and blasted walls, the miles and miles of martyred Land, that had been happy Germany, and in the name of Christendom, inviting us to become fools like they themselves, and to forsake all that we hold as Truth now and forever; the vision of the felling of the great holy woods — ten thousand trees a day — and of the factories blown up or steadily dismantled and bit by bit carried away; and above all, more sinister than all[,] and more heart-rending, day after day, for months unending, the news of the infamous Trial[3] — of the long torture of the Twenty-One, and of the condemnation on that most shameful day in all the long life of the West,[4] — and then, in the dim light of the following morning, the vision that will stay vivid within our hearts until we die, a thing of indignation and of horror: fluttering in the wind, the bodies of the best of those who, at Thy side, had led the German Nation along the way of pride![5]

The vision of the end of all we loved and wanted; of all we hade been living for; the knowledge that, in the wide world, that we had nearly conquered, there was no hope of our return to power, nay, no place for us ever more!

Our truth might win, one day, but when? In the meantime, Thy hallowed Reich lay torn and devastated; Thy greatest followers were dead or in captivity; Thy people hated; Rebels against the downward rush of Time, all those who still revered Thee, were

---

[3] The Nuremberg War Crimes Tribunal.

[4] Savitri is referring to the 15th and 16th of October 1946.

[5] Exclamation point added in Typescript B. Paragraph break retained from Typescript A.

foreigners in every clime; exiles upon this earth, if not, with fury unabated, crushed in the name of "liberty."

How long? How long would all this last? No one could tell. Apparently, for every one of us, this world had become hell, and was to remain so, forever. But when Thy foes cried out to us: "Give up your Leader's Faith, and take to ours and be free to come and go, to buy and sell, to speak and write!" we answered: "Never! Disciples of the Child of Light whether in ruin or in glory, faithful to Him whatever you might say or do,— 'faithful when all become unfaithful'—we [would] rather die with Him than rule with you! We [would] rather be defeated, knowing we fought for what is right, than share the comforts of the fools whom Israel has cheated; we [would] rather sink into the starless night of dreary day-to-day oblivion, knowing ourselves to be without fault in our Leader's sight, than yield to you and share your hated might!"

❖ ❖ ❖

The long nightmare dragged on and on . . . But in its midst, though not a ray of hope had shone,—though we knew not whether we were again ever to rise,—our will to stand in spite of all against the money-power, and to resist; our will never to compromise, was like a ray of fire; a ray of fire in the dark night before dawn.

15. Savitri Devi, London, 1946

Chapter 13

1948

"... die Menschen gehen nicht an ver-
lorenen Kriegen zugrunde, sondern am
Verlust jener Widerstandskraft, die nur
dem reinen Blute zu eigen ist."

—*Mein Kampf*[1]

Ruins, ruins, and still more ruins . . . unending rows of crum-
bling walls; deserted streets in which lay heaps of wreckage;
stations of which the charred and gaping halls, open to wind
and rain, led out to further sights of devastation; and in the
midst of all that desolation, the haggard faces of Thy country-
men: of those who to the bitter end, had fought for Greater
Germany her power to retain, for us to behold, under Thy
strong protection, the long-awaited Western Resurrection; thus
stretched over hundreds of miles before my eyes, the torn and
bleeding body of Thy Nation. Under the purple glow of dawn
or sunset, under the phosphorescent light of the full moon, un-
der the lonely Crescent in the midst of cloudy sky, under the
splendour of the starry night, always and everywhere the same
heart-rending sight: ruins, ruins and further ruins; all that was
left of Thy proud Reich; all that was left of Thy great life's crea-
tion; all that was left of Thy astounding might!

---

[1] "... men do not perish from lost wars, but from the loss of that
power of resistance that only pure blood possesses" (*Mein Kampf*, p.
324, trans. R. G. Fowler).

My Leader! Thou hadst seen, with Thy own eyes, those towns ablaze; and Thou hadst seen the charred[2] walls still smouldering, the twisted iron bars still hot, the very earth itself, soaked through and through[3] with phosphorus, still burning on, for days and days; and Thou hadst seen the corpses of Thy people — those who loved and trusted Thee, and whom Thou lovedst — stuck in the molten tar of those now long-deserted streets, in which they had just met a most appalling fate; and from the cellars, thou hadst smellt the stench of death!

Who can, in any tongue, relate Thy immeasurable torment?

In a flash, wherever I went, I pictured to[4] myself Thy worn and tragic Face against the background of that horror brought upon Thy dear Germany by the enemies of our race and their allies, the traitors, slaves of Jews. My heart full of relentless hate, I saw, in the very midst of her towns in ashes, their brand new, vulgar "Clubs of Victory," and, before Thy famishing people, their soldiers revelling in gluttony and luxury. And every day I heard[5] the self-same news: systematic destruction of everything Thou hadst done; further death-sentences against Thy true disciples, and further misery, and further humiliation for all those who, along with them, along with Thee, had fought under the blood-red Banner, bearing the most-holy Wheel of the Sun.

❖ ❖ ❖

"Ruins, ruins and further ruins," thought I, as I went[6] by; "Years more of persecution, years more of martyrdom, but resurrection, and sure and terrible revenge, and lasting domination — in the long run!"

---

[2] Replacing "calcinated" with "charred." "Calcinated" is not an English word. Savitri was almost certainly thinking of the French adjective "*calciné*," meaning charred, incinerated, burnt to a crisp.

[3] The words "and through" were omitted in Typescript B.

[4] The word "in" in Typescript A is changed to "to" in Typescript B.

[5] In Typescript B, "I heard" is added.

[6] In Typescript B, "went" replaces "stood" from Typescript A.

Oh, why had I not come before, and been, along those streets now desolate and silent, one of the millions who had greeted Thee, in Thy great days of undisputed rule, before the war? Why had I not, at least, arrived[7] in time to fight in Thy own Land, among Thy beloved people, in defence of Thy everlasting Principles and of Thy might? – I, who had loved Thee so much more, than many of those who had seen the glory that was Thine! But now that all lay waste in mud and gore, I knew I was to be a Sign; a fiery Song of hope amidst despair, a Voice amidst the ruins; within the nightmare horror of the present fall, the shadow of the unexpected future, and its living call.[8] I was to stand in the sunshine, and tell Thy wounded Germany – the mute[9] thousands who still believed in Thee, and even those who now no longer did – that Thou wast right in spite of all.

And lo, as I obeyed the deep inner dictate[10] of love and faith, and went about from place to place, first-fruits of the religious reverence of distant men of Aryan race towards both them and Thee, and whispered to Thy people at my side, however late, the mystic words of confidence and pride, I saw many a tired face look passionately up to me, as though, beyond the rows and rows of shattered walls and wreckage; and all the humiliation of the passing hour, the ardent eyes could clearly see, thanks to the magic of my message, the unbelievable return of old prosperity and power.

And as I put into their hand my written exhortation to stubborn day-to-day resistance, and quietly went on to do the same, numberless times again, throughout the Land, their glance would follow me with sympathy into the distance, and their heart would be with me wherever I would go. Not one of them

---

[7] Following Typescript B. In Typescript A, this reads "Why could I not, at least, arrive in time . . ."

[8] The words "and its living call" were omitted in Typescript B.

[9] Replacing "dumb" with "mute" to prevent a misunderstanding of Savitri's intended meaning.

[10] In Typescript A "inner call." In Typescript B "deep inner dictate."

betrayed me, even though they knew our persecutors would surely pay them well for doing so. In midst of utter destitution and hunger they had lived already three long years; but even so, there was no such reward, no such temptation, as could prompt them to help the standing foe[11] against the faithful friend. And lo, brushing aside all fears, they took me under their protection, and I would come and I would go, safe in the midst of hell, and keep on bearing witness to Thy glory: of all Thy eighty million countrymen not one would tell the enemy what I had said or done; and all was well.

16. Savitri in Alfeld an der Leine, Lower Saxony, 5 December 1948

How many times have I not then, with tears, standing before the ruins, thought of Thy Reich of recent years! How many times have I not, then, remembered the glorious weeks, when, from the remote East, my mind and heart rushed forth to meet Thy coming host! Now that Thy Land in ashes lay dismembered,—four hated victors' prey; now that, outwardly, all was lost, I had arrived at last from far away, to fight and wait amidst the common hardships and the common dangers,—I, the least among Thy faithful ones,—day after day. And of Thy starving countrymen,—of those now silent eighty million, whose voice had cheered Thee in the past—not a single one had been willing my humble effort to betray!

Even more so than in the days of glory, I loved them; nay[12]

---

[11] Deleting a superfluous "against" followed by a comma.

[12] The word "nay" was omitted in Typescript B.

even more so than when, along the way to [the] snow-clad Caucasus and to the Caspian, Thy armies marched in conquering array; even more so than when I had awaited their coming through the Khyber Pass.

For three long years, with fury unabated, the evil Jewish force had sought to crush that spirit which had wrought such wonders in Thy name. But I had come and I had fought only to see, erect and free, in faces emaciated, in thousands of proud eyes radiated, fearless and without blame, the German Soul, always the same.

And suddenly, as in a dream, my mind flew back to one great scene twenty-four centuries ago: on his death-bed in Babylon, I heard the Prince of Macedon tell coming generations the Gods' decree that they should know, and give "the worthiest," once and for all, the domination of the world.

And from the bottom of my heart, in boundless admiration, I hailed in those who stood the test, "the worthiest" in the full sense of Alexander's word, and in thy superhuman Nation, the future ruler of the West.

17. Savitri Devi with unidentified friends, Stockholm, May 1948

Chapter 14

1949

"Allein unser Denken und Handeln soll
keineswegs von Beifall oder Ablehnung
unserer Zeit bestimmt werden, sondern
von der bindenden Verpflichtung an eine
Wahrheit, die wir erkannten."

— *Mein Kampf*[1]

"VERSE" VERSION FROM TYPESCRIPT A

Of all ambitions in the world, there is no higher one
than that of being, in these times of trial,
one of the few, whose self-denial,
will help to clear the Way for Thy return;
one of the unknown few, who burn
with love and hate,
as ardently as ever,
and stand by Thee alone, against an evil fate;
one of Thy Dedicated ones, who stubbornly remain
upon the field, when all is lost,
however much they might yet have to learn,
however much they yet might have to wait,
determined to begin again

---

[1] "Yet our thoughts and actions should in no way be determined
by the approval or disapproval of our time, but by our bound duty to
a truth we have recognized" (*Mein Kampf*, p. 435, trans. R. G. Fowler).

by any means, at any cost,
knowing it is never too late.

Of all the pleasures in the world, there is no greater one
than to defy Thy enemies,
whether in broad daylight or secret action,
and to proclaim, against the overwhelming might
both of the Red Front and Reaction,
that Thou wast always right.
There is no greater satisfaction
than to behold the growing misery
of that despicable humanity
that hated Thee so readily,
and fought but yesterday against our Creed of life;
to feel that their short victory
has brought nothing but further strife
between the Jews' allies.
There is, at present, no delight
as thrilling as to see their former block[2] divided,
and to hope that one day,
one will look at them fight,
and as to know that while the fools
that so long were the Jews' best tools
will die during the Third World War,
Thy faithful few shall lead the Second Struggle
for freedom and for might,
and rise and rule upon the ruins of the world
forever,
in the glory of Thy Light!
Firm in one's faith in Thee, that no power can shatter,
when one shows *that*,
what can all the rest matter?

And even if our final Day
were not to come in one's lifetime,
still one would have the holy Joy
of duty done and of lasting defiance;

---

[2] Typescript B reads "camp."

still one would be, in spite of all,
among the Strong, among the Free,
who scorn the degrading alliance
with the Dark Forces;
still one would feel proud of one's place
among the fighters for one's race,
unwavering, like any one of them,
in one's limitless love of Thee
that nothing mars;
in spite of persecution, free;
free, even behind prison bars.

❖ ❖ ❖

Thus did I feel, when in my cell,
I worked and sang and wrote.
My cell was small. The sky was bright.
From its blue aether, so remote,
as He pursued His daily course,
the Sun, through the high window,
projected slowly moving lines of light,
upon the wall.
And I was happy. All was well,
thought I, as long as I could write;
also, as long as I could see,
now and then for a while or two,
the best of all the women who
were there with me,
only for having loved and served the Truth and Thee.[3]

Beyond the iron bars and the high walls,
beyond the heavy prison doors,
in the struggling world of the free
men came and went, and children played;
and fruit trees blossomed, and green fields
and woods displayed
their splendour in the spring sunshine;

---

[3] Hertha Ehlert.

while just as beautiful as in the days
Thy people greeted Thee with outstretched arms,
between its smiling hills
on flowed the sacred Rhine.
Over the charred and crumbling stones
that had been walls of happy homes,
regardless of the work of strife
wrought by the Jewish powers,
tender green creeper with pink flowers
grew as a glaring Sign of everlasting Life.
And in the devastated forests,
from the live roots of every fallen tree,
new shoots full of fresh sap took birth,
and thrived invincibly
out of Germany's holy earth.

But happier, in spite of all,
than anyone in the broad world,
happy in the communion
of our unchanging love of Thee,
were I, and She.

We talked of nothing but the splendid Days
in which Thou wast all-powerful;
also of those, equally beautiful,
in which Thou willst return.
And we were happy in the praise
of all Thou art and all that Thou hast done;
in the anticipation
of the final annihilation
of all the forces that stood in Thy way;
of those who brought disaster on Thy Nation;
and in the hope we shall, one day,
witness Thy enemies crushed in their turn.
As I beheld the warrior's Wife,
the worthy Daughter of Thy Land,
I felt that I had fought, and loved and waited all my life,
to earn the privilege of holding out my hand

to her, within that prison cell.
In her blue eyes shone all the pride
of those who struggled on Thy side
for these last thirty years,
and who have now, in man-made hell,
retained unflinchingly
their faith in Thee;
while in my dark eyes full of fire
and full of tears,
forgotten centuries of yearning
for living earthly Godhead in its strength and beauty,
told the martyr of Duty
my endless admiration,
while drowning the long wail
of misery present and past,
rang in my voice a hymn of triumph;
a whole world's future adoration:
the Joy of Aryan man
standing by Thee of his own choice,
hailing in Thy fair people
his age-old Gods in flesh and blood, —
one day, at last!
And we were happy till the day the enemy discovered
our secret meetings in my cell,
and separated us — for how long? Who can tell?

❖ ❖ ❖

For however long it might be,
nothing can shake or lessen
the faith of both of us in Thee.
And nothing also can destroy,
nothing can even slacken
the holy bond of comradeship
now linking her to me.

Whether still behind iron bars,
or wandering upon this sunlit earth
that Money mars,

so long [as] Thy spirit has not won —
so long [as] the Gods invisible
have not yet ordered Thy return —
neither of us, and none of those
who like us lived and fought for Thee
can now ever again be free
save in the realm inviolate
of Will and Thought, of Love and Hate;
so long [as] our second Day of Power
has not yet dawned upon Thy Land,
we are all prisoners, whatever we might do
in this wide Earth, wherever we might stand;
but prisoners who know
that they shall one day be
the rulers of a reborn world
with Thee, through Thee, for Thee,
and beyond Thee, for that true Race of gods:
that coming Aryan mankind which is Thine,
— and mine.

United in our love of Thee
forever and forever,
both I and she,
and everyone who walks along our Way
shall keep on fighting for the resurrection
not only of Thy Nation
but of that further Aryan Reich that has no boundaries;
shall keep on fighting to be free
in our own world, and waiting for Thy Day.

"PROSE" VERSION FROM TYPESCRIPT B

Of all ambitions in the world there is no higher one than that of being, in these times of trial, one of the few whose self-denial will help to clear the way for Thy return; one of the unknown few who burn with love and hate, as ardently as ever, and stand by Thee alone against an evil fate; one of Thy dedicated ones who stubbornly remain upon the field when all is lost, however much they might yet have to learn, however much they might yet have to wait, determined to begin again, by any means, at any cost, knowing it is never too late.

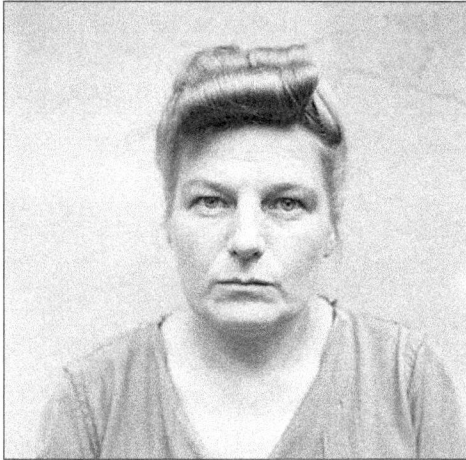

18. Hertha Ehlert in 1945

Of all the pleasures in the world there is no greater one than to defy Thy enemies, whether in broad daylight or secret action, and to proclaim, against the overwhelming might both of the Red Front and Reaction, that Thou wast always right. There is no greater satisfaction than to behold the growing misery of that despicable humanity that hated Thee so readily, and fought but yesterday against our creed of life, to feel that their short victory has brought nothing but further strife between Jews' allies. There is at present no delight so thrilling as to see their camp divided, and to hope that, one day, one will look at them fight, and as to know that while the fools, who were so long the Jew's best tools, will die during the Third World War, Thy faithful few will lead the Second Struggle for freedom and for might, and rise and rule, upon the ruins of the world — forever, in the glory of Thy light!

Firm in one's faith in Thee, that no power can shatter, when one shows *that*, what can all the rest matter?

And even if our final Day were not to come in one's lifetime, still one would have the holy joy of Duty done and of lasting defiance; still one would be, in spite of all, among the strong, among the free, who scorn the degrading alliance of the Dark forces; still one would feel proud of one's place among the fighters for the honour of the Aryan race — unwavering like any one of them, in one's limitless love of Thee, that nothing mars; free, even behind prison bars.

❖ ❖ ❖

Thus did I feel while in my cell I worked and sang, and wrote. My cell was small. The sky, was bright. From its blue aether, so remote, as He pursued His daily course[,] The Sun, through the high window, projected slowly moving lines of light, upon the wall. And I was happy. All was well, thought I, as long as I could write, — also, as long as I could see, now and then, the best one of all the women who, with me, were there for having loved and served the truth and Thee.

Beyond the iron bars and the high walls, beyond the heavy prison doors, in the struggling world of the free, men came and went and children played; and fruit trees blossomed and green fields and woods displayed their splendour in the spring sun-shine, while, just as beautiful as in the days Thy people greeted Thee with arms outstretched, between its smiling hills, on flowed the sacred Rhine. Over the charred and crumbling stones, that had been walls of happy homes, regardless of the work of strife wrought by the Jewish powers, tender green creeper with pink flowers grew as a glaring Sign of everlasting

Life. And in the devastated forests, from the live roots of every fallen tree, new shoots full of fresh sap took birth, and thrived invincibly, out of Germany's holy earth.

But happier, in spite of all, than anyone in the broad outer world — happy in the communion of our unchanging love of Thee — were I and she.

We talked of nothing but the splendid days in which Thou wast all-powerful, and those even more beautiful in which Thou willst return. And we were happy in the praise of all Thou art and all that Thou hast done; in the anticipation of the final annihilation of all the forces that stood in Thy way, and brought disaster on thy Nation, in the hope that we shall, one day witness Thy enemies crushed in their turn.

As I beheld the warrior's wife, the worthy daughter of Thy Land, I felt that I had fought and loved and waited all my life, to earn the privilege of holding out my hand to her within that prison cell. In her blue eyes shone all the pride of those who struggled on Thy side for these last thirty years and who have now, in man-made hell, retained unflinchingly their faith in Thee, while in my dark eyes full of fire and tears, forgotten centuries of yearning for living earthly godhead in its strength and beauty, told the martyr of Duty all my unending admiration, while in my voice, drowning the wail of misery present and past, rang as a hymn of triumph, a whole world's future adoration: the happiness of Aryan man standing by Thee of his own choice, hailing, in Thy fair people, his age-old gods in flesh and blood, — one day, at last!

And we were happy till the day the enemy discovered our secret meetings in my cell, and separated us — for how long? Who can tell?

❖ ❖ ❖

For however long it might be, nothing can shake or lessen the faith of both of us in Thee. And nothing also can destroy, nothing can slacken, the holy bond of Comradeship now linking her to me.

Whether still behind iron bars, or wandering upon this sunlit earth that Money mars, so long [as] Thy spirit has not won, — so long [as] the Gods invisible have not ordered Thy return, — neither of us, and none of those who, like us, lived and fought for Thee, can now ever again be free, save in the realm inviolate of will and thought, of love and hate. So long [as] our second Day has not yet dawned upon Thy Land, we are all prisoners, whatever we might do in this wide world, wherever we might stand. But prisoners who know that they shall one day be the rulers of a reborn world, with Thee, through Thee, for Thee, and beyond Thee, for that true race of Gods: that coming Aryan mankind which is Thine — and mine.

United in our love of Thee forever and forever, she and I, and all those who walk along our Way, will keep on fighting for the resurrection of the great Reich, and waiting for Thy Day.

19. Hertha Ehlert in the 1960s, courtesy of Beryl Cheetham

Chapter 15

1951

"Die Richter dieses Staates mögen uns
ruhig ob unseres damaligen Handelns
verurteilen, die Geschichte als Göttin
einer höheren Wahrheit und eines bes-
seren Rechtes, sie wird dennoch dereinst
dieses Urteil lächelnd zerreißen, um uns
alle freizusprechen von Schuld und Feh-
le."

— *Mein Kampf* [1]

Full of bitterness of deeds bygone, full of the distant rumblings of the coming storm, six gloomy years had rolled into the past. One could have thought the victors had, at last, renounced their frenzied lure of persecution; that after all the stupid fury that had been released, their lust of murder was appeased. One could have thought that sense of growing danger would incite to reason. One could have thought the men whose treason to their own race had brought about the fall of Thy great Reich, and silenced our conquering war-songs for a time, even if they have not as yet become aware of their delusion, would hesitate before committing their most abominable crime.

---

[1] "The judges of this state may calmly condemn us for our previous deeds, but History, as goddess of a higher truth and a better justice, will one day smile as she tears up this verdict and acquits us of all fault and responsibility" (*Mein Kampf*, p. 780, trans. R. G. Fowler).

And yet, in spite of the outcry of grief and indignation that sprang from every German heart, at the news of the foe's decision; in spite of restless crowds around the Landsberg prison; in spite of my own pathetic appeal to those who should have had more vision, and all I did to win the right to die in the place of the Seven Heroes, nothing could stop the frightful wheel of Destiny from rolling by.[2]

And one by one out of their cells, they walked calm and upright, knowing they were to meet their doom. And with Thy holy Name and that of Germany upon their lips, and with the love of Thee, always the same, within their hearts, and with the inspired flame of pride within their tearless eyes so bright; with the serenity of duty done, and with the awareness of reconquered power, and of the glory they had won during those six long years of gloom, and of the immortality that now began for them in that atrocious hour, one by one they were hanged — in alphabetic order, first six, then five, then four, then three, then two, and at last one, fearlessly waiting for their turn.

And thus they passed into eternal light, last martyrs of the first phase of the Struggle for freedom and for might, and first ones of its second phase; heralds of Dawn, proclaiming Thy return — whether in spirit only or in flesh also, it matters little — from the midst of our present plight, upon that tragic late-spring night.

❖ ❖ ❖

Wherever Thou might be on this earth, or in the radiant Dwellings of heroes ever young and strong and free, my Leader — our Leader — dost Thou know the last part of the story of the seven

---

[2] Savitri is referring to the last seven executions of Germans convicted of war crimes in the Second World War. The executions took place in the early morning hours of 8 June 1951 at the Landsberg am Lech prison where Adolf Hitler had been incarcerated in 1924 after the Beer Hall *Putsch*. For more on this topic, see Savitri Devi, *Pilgrimage* (Calcutta: Savitri Devi Mukherji, 1958), ch. 6, "Landsberg am Lech."

Martyrs who have loved Thee so? Dost Thou know how they died for Greater Germany to rise out of tomorrow's war and chaos, and rule the West forever in Thy name? Along the path out of these days of trial, once more to domination and to fame, they walk in spirit at the head of us who have been Thine, and Thine remain.

They walk ahead of us and guide us unfailingly to the one goal: the resurrection of Thy Reich as Thou hast dreamed it: one State, one People, and one Leader; one blood, one heart, one conquering will; one super-human Soul.

No more than the Sixteen blood-witnesses of early days and the Eleven of Nuremberg, whom we revere and praise; no more than all Thy faithful ones, who died for Germany to raise the holy Swastika high above every Sign in space and time, did the exalted Seven give up their lives in vain. They died for us to conquer; for Thee to come again; for Germany to live — and reign.

20. Savitri Devi, September 1951, Lyons

Chapter 16

1953

"PROSE" VERSION

"... die Menschen gehen nicht an ver-
lorenen Kriegen zugrunde, sondern am
Verlust jener Widerstandskraft, die nur
dem reinen Blute zu eigen ist."

—*Mein Kampf*[1]

"Ein Staat, der im Zeitalter der Rassen-
vergiftung sich der Pflege seiner besten
rassischen Elemente widmet, muß eines
Tages zum Herrn der Erde werden."

—*Mein Kampf*[2]

And time rolls on . . . and every empty day that slowly fades
away, as uneventful as any other one, into the mist of unre-
corded history, brings us, along our strenuous way, nearer the
heart's desire of the revengeful, nearer the doom of those

---

[1] "... men perish not from lost wars, but from the loss of that
power of resistance found only in pure blood" (*Mein Kampf*, p. 324,
trans. R. G. Fowler).

[2] "A state that, in an age of racial-poisoning, dedicates itself to fos-
tering its best racial elements must one day become master of the
earth" (*Mein Kampf*, p. 782, trans. R. G. Fowler).

whom we resist, nearer the unfailing end of this atrocious night, nearer the yet well-hidden goal for which we fight, — the one unchanging[3] dream for which we live, while we never forget, never forgive.

And time rolls on . . . and every dreary hour that passes by into eternity, glaringly shows the soundness of our claim, and tells the world the inanity of Thy enemies' victory, while bringing Thy dismembered Nation new strength and new prosperity, new hopes of unity, with the increasing certainty of our return to power, and *both* our persecutors further fears of unavoidable annihilation.

And thus we march invincibly towards our lofty Aim, along the Way of blood and tears. It matters not what price[4] we gave, it matters not what price[5] we shall yet give, to see all those who hated Thee descend into the grave after they groan under our whip for years and years, — while[6] we never forget, never forgive.

And time rolls on . . . and every passing[7] second brings us further away from the long nightmare of defeat; nearer the glory of our dawning Day; nearer the time we shall begin again; nearer the morn of Thy unending reign, when Thy adoring People will[8] repeat the now forbidden words of faith and pride in frenzied spell-like cheers,[9] and when, for countless scores of years, the nations of the West that have refused to side with Thee, and fight the common foe, and live, will lie in ruins at our feet, — while we never forget, never forgive.

---

[3] In *And Time Rolls On* "unchanging" is replaced by "undying."

[4] In *And Time Rolls On* "what price" is replaced by "how much."

[5] In *And Time Rolls On* "what price" is replaced by "how much."

[6] In *And Time Rolls On* "while" is replaced by "for."

[7] In *And Time Rolls On* "passing" is replaced by "fleeting."

[8] In *And Time Rolls On* "shall" replaces "will."

[9] In *And Time Rolls On* this reads, "when Thy adoring people shall repeat, in frenzied, spell-like cheers, the now forbidden words of faith and pride."

And time rolls on . . . With us, they had not reckoned,[10] when setting forth their vast utopian schemes. They thought Thee dead, and us also; they thought our faith had slackened; they thought, — the fools — they[11] could rely upon our loyalties to values which we hate; they thought they could send us to die, without us ever asking why, while[12] we had grown too weary to say "no." They thought they had become the masters of our fate; but[13] here we rise, and here we stand, and give the world to understand that we shall never fight but for our same old dreams:[14] for honour and for might, and what we know is right; for the joy of asserting the privileges of our birth; for Thee, for Greater Germany, for Aryan rule upon this earth — the Gospel of perennial Truth in its new form, which we came to proclaim, and, which is more, to live, while we never forget, never forgive.

And time rolls on . . . Nothing can break our spirit, nor alter our allegiance to Thee and to the German Reich, home of the best, stronghold and hope of Aryan mankind in the West. Of all Thy enemies might[15] say or do to gain our favour that they so require, nothing can shake our faith, nothing can ever mar our loyalty to the old oath; nothing can kill our will to rise again. Every new step the former "great Allies" take towards us we meet with a new grievance; no threat can force us to believe their lies; no bribery can keep our hearts from hating both.[16]

Happier as the storm draws nigh, we wait and watch events go by . . . We wait and watch the signs of war — the hopes of liberation; the coming chances of Thy Nation to seize the lead of Sunset Lands once more. And we are confident in our own

---

[10] In *And Time Rolls On* "did not reckon."
[11] In *And Time Rolls On* a "that" appears before "they."
[12] In *And Time Rolls On* "when."
[13] In *And Time Rolls On* "and" is replaced by "but."
[14] In *And Time Rolls On* "dreams" appears as "dream."
[15] In *And Time Rolls On* "might" is replaced by "can."
[16] In *And Time Rolls On* "both" is emphasized.

strength and we are grateful to the immortal Gods Who made us free, serene even in hell and loving only Thee, having nothing to lose and all to give—faithful when all become unfaithful, while we never forget, never forgive.

21. Savitri Devi photographed in Germany sometime between 1953 and 1957

"VERSE" VERSION

"... die Menschen gehen nicht an ver-
lorenen Kriegen zugrunde, sondern am
Verlust jener Widerstandskraft, die nur
dem reinen Blute zu eigen ist."

— *Das Buch*[17]

And time rolls on ... And every empty day
that slowly fades away,
as uneventful
as any other one, into the mist
of unrecorded history,
brings us, along our strenuous Way,
nearer the heart's desire of the revengeful,
nearer the doom of those whom we resist,
nearer the unfailing end of this atrocious night,
nearer the yet well-hidden goal for which we fight—
the one unchanging dream, for which we live—
... while we never forget, never forgive!

And time rolls on ... And every dreary hour
that passes by into eternity,
glaringly shows the soundness of our claim,
and tells the world the inanity of Thy enemies' victory,
while bringing Thy dismembered Nation
new strength and new prosperity,
new hopes of unity,
with the increasing certainty
of our return to power ...
and *both* our persecutors further fears
of unavoidable annihilation.

---

[17] "... men perish not from lost wars, but from the loss of that
power of resistance found only in pure blood" (*Mein Kampf*, p. 324,
trans. R. G. Fowler).

And thus we march invincibly
towards our lofty aim,
along the Way of blood and tears.
It matters not what price[18] we gave,
it matters not what price[19] we shall yet give,
to see all those who hated Thee descend into the grave
after they groan under our whip for years and years . . .
while[20] we never forget, never forgive!

And time rolls on . . . And every passing[21] second
brings us further away
from the long nightmare of defeat;
nearer the glory of our dawning Day;
nearer the time we shall begin again;
nearer the morn of Thy unending Reign,
when Thy adoring people will[22] repeat
the now forbidden words of faith and pride
in frenzied, spell-like cheers;[23]
and when, for countless scores of years,
the nations of the West that have refused to side
with Thee, and fight the common foe, and live,
will lie in ruins at our feet —
while we never forget, never forgive!

And time rolls on . . . With us, they had not reckoned,[24]
when setting forth their vast utopian schemes;
They thought Thee dead, and us also;
They thought our faith had slackened;
They thought — the fools! — they[25] could rely

---

[18] In *And Time Rolls On* "what price" is replaced by "how much."
[19] In *And Time Rolls On* "what price" is replaced by "how much."
[20] In *And Time Rolls On* "for" replaces "while."
[21] In *And Time Rolls On* "passing" is replaced by "fleeting."
[22] In *And Time Rolls On* "shall" replaces "will."
[23] In *And Time Rolls On* this reads, "when Thy adoring people shall repeat, in frenzied, spell-like cheers, the now forbidden words of faith and pride."
[24] In *And Time Rolls On* "did not reckon."

upon our loyalties to values which we hate.
They thought they could send us to die
without us ever asking why,
while[26] we had grown too weary to say "No!"
They thought they had become the masters of our fate . . .
But[27] here we rise, and here we stand,
and give the world to understand
that we shall never fight
but for our same old dream:
for honour and for might,
and what we know is right;
for the joy of asserting the privileges of our birth;
for Thee; for Greater Germany; for Aryan rule upon this
    earth—
the Gospel of perennial Truth in its new Form, which we came
to proclaim,
and, which is more, to live . . .
while we never forget, never forgive!

And time rolls on . . . Nothing can break our spirit,
nor alter our allegiance
to Thee, and to the German Reich, Home of the Best,
stronghold and hope of Aryan mankind in the West.
Of all Thy enemies might[28] say or do to gain
our favour, that they so require,
nothing can shake our faith,
nothing can ever mar
our loyalty to the old Oath;
nothing can kill our will to rise again.
Every new step the former "great Allies"
take towards us, we meet with a new grievance;
No threat can force us to believe their lies.
No bribery can keep our hearts from hating *both*.

---

[25] In *And Time Rolls On* a "that" appears before "they."
[26] In *And Time Rolls On* "when."
[27] In *And Time Rolls On* "and" is replaced by "but."
[28] In *And Time Rolls On* "might" is replaced by "can."

Happier as the storm draws nigh,
we wait, and watch events go by . . .
We wait, and watch the signs of war: —
the hopes of liberation;
the coming chances of Thy Nation
to seize the lead of Sunset Lands once more.
And we are confident in our own strength,
and we are grateful
to the immortal Gods, Who made us free,
serene, even in hell, and loving only Thee;
having nothing to lose, and all to give;
"faithful, when all become unfaithful" —
while we never forget, never forgive!

Savitri Devi

Written in Athens, 26 March 1953

Appendix

IN MEMORY OF
MAY 1ST, 1945

22. "Verlorene Heimat" (Lost Homeland) by Thomas Riß

In Memory of
May 1st, 1945

Great Eagle, fold your wings awhile
      And turn away your eyes;
In smoke and thunder, flame and blood
      Your Best and Highest dies;
      And all His happy Land,
          His great emprise,
A shattered wreck of ugly ruin lies.

Great Eagle, flee a little while
      To some far lonely height.
      There shall you watch and wait . . .
      Your land is sunk in night:
      All, all those cities bright
In ruins far and wide torment the night.

Oh Eagle, did you hear that shout,
      That thundered triple roar?
Its clamourous echoes smote the earth
      And rolled from shore to shore;
      And all the glorious Dead,
      Who fealty swore,
Received Him home; His earthly flight is o'er.

His fight, that made the nations shake,
      And hearts and pulses leap,
      Is over now. He rests. But we
      Are sunk in anguish deep.
      He rests,—at last. No dreams
      Torture His sleep,
While grave-eyed Angel-guards their watches keep.

Great Eagle, that He worked to save,
      And fought to guard, — and died,
Flee from this piteous German wreck,
      In some far corner hide,
      Until the Land is free
      And far and wide,
Throughout the world His name is glorified!

Meanwhile, *we* hold the heights He won,
      And keep His torch aflame;
No slothful ease for us who bear
      The honour of His name.
      To do His work we count
      Higher than fame,
Indifferent to earthly praise or blame.

Clara Sharland

In memory of May 1st 1945

Great Eagle, fold your wings awhile
    And turn away your eyes;
In smoke and thunder, flame and blood
      Your Best and Highest dies,
      And all His happy Land,
        His great emprise,
A shattered wreck of ugly ruin lies.

Great Eagle, flee a little while
      To some far lonely height.
      There shall you watch and wait...
      Your Land is sunk in night:
      All, all those cities bright
In ruins far and wide torment the night.

Oh Eagle, did you hear that shout,
      That thundered triple roar?
Its clamourous echoes smote the earth
      And rolled from shore to shore;
      And all the glorious Dead,
      Who fealty swore,
Received Him home; His earthly fight is o'er.

His fight, that made the nations shake,
      And hearts and pulses leap,
      Is over now. He rests. But we
      Are sunk in anguish deep.
      He rests,__at last. No dreams
      Torture His sleep,
While grave-eyed Angel-guards their watches keep.

Great Eagle, that He worked to save,
      And fought to guard,__and died,
Flee from this piteous German wreck,
      In some far corner hide,
      Until the Land is free
      And far and wide,
Throughout the world His name is glorified!

23. Page 1 of the original typescript of "In Memory of May 1st, 1945"

Meanwhile, we hold the heights He won,
    And keep His torch aflame;
No slothful ease for us who bear
    The honour of His name.
    To do His work we count
    Higher than fame,
Indifferent to earthly praise or blame.

Clara Shearland

24. Page 2 of the original typescript of "In Memory of May 1st, 1945"

In Memory of May 1st, 1945

EDITOR'S AFTERWORD

"In Memory of May 1st, 1945" is a poem of mourning and hope: mourning for Adolf Hitler, who committed suicide on 30 April 1945; hope for Germany, for National Socialism, and for the Aryan race, all of which lived on to the next day. The poem subtly emphasizes hope over mourning by commemorating not the day of Hitler's death, but the day after.

The capitalized pronouns "He" and "His" refer to Adolf Hitler. The "Great Eagle" seems, in the third and fourth stanzas, to refer to Hitler as well: "His earthly flight is o'er" and "His fight, that made the nations shake." But in the fifth stanza, Hitler and the eagle are distinct: "Great Eagle, that He worked to save,/And fought to guard,—and died."

The Great Eagle seems to be identified with Germany. This impression, however, seems to be contradicted later in the fifth stanza, where the author bids the Great Eagle to "Flee from this piteous German wreck,/In some far corner hide,/Until the Land is free."

Could the Great Eagle be the Aryan Race that Hitler fought to save? This seems unlikely, since the Aryan race numbers hundreds of millions of people, spread out over the earth. It could not "flee a little while/To some far lonely height" or "Flee from this piteous German wreck,/In some far corner hide." Even taking into account the metaphorical nature of poetry, this seems farfetched.

What, then, is this Great Eagle that is identical to Adolf Hitler during his lifetime, yet survived his death, if it is not Germany herself or the Aryan race? A reasonable hypothesis is that the Great Eagle is National Socialism, seen as an idea and a movement that transcends its particular German embodiment, the NSDAP. And, indeed, the eagle is an ancient symbol of the German Reich: Charlemagne's First Reich, the Second Reich of 1871–1918, and Hitler's Third Reich. Thus it is natural to identify the eagle with National Socialism, which was the animating principle of the Third Reich but also a philosophy whose import and applicability extended beyond its borders.

The sixth and final stanza, however, throws some doubt on the identification of the Great Eagle and National Socialism. Its first word is "Meanwhile," and it deals with the duties of faithful National Socialists while the Great Eagle is resting and waiting. Perhaps, then, the Great Eagle refers only to the glorious, outward, public manifestations of National Socialism. After Hitler's downfall, these outward manifestations would have to be replaced by the quiet, anonymous, clandestine work to lay the groundwork for a new struggle, a new accession to power, a new régime, and new glories.

The task of the loyal remnant is to "hold the heights He won,/And keep His torch aflame;/No slothful ease for us who bear/The honour of His name." In the aftermath of defeat, the "heights He won" cannot be territory. They must refer to the truths Hitler preached and the fervor he kindled. His "torch" — another important National Socialist symbol — blazes with enlightenment and enthusiasm, and it is the task of post-war National Socialists to carry his torch and pass on the flame.

During Hitler's struggle for power, there were great dangers and few rewards for being a National Socialist, and the movement could be sustained only by disinterested idealists who would pursue the true and the good, regardless of personal consequences. When Hitler ruled Germany, however, being a National Socialist became less dangerous and more advantageous, and the ranks of the party were swelled by opportunists. Now, the day after Hitler's death, his work will be carried on again only by disinterested idealists: "To do His work we count/Higher than fame,/Indifferent to earthly praise or blame."

❖ ❖ ❖

On 14 September 2004, I found a typescript of "In Memory of May 1st, 1945," along with a carbon copy, in a folder containing a number of letters written by Savitri Devi to Miriam Hirn, a younger French friend in New Delhi. Also in the folder was a copy of Savitri's poem "1953." Miss Hirn, who had collected the documents together, had been entrusted with Savitri's papers and effects when she left India in 1981, never to return.

The accompanying documents, and the fact that the poet's name, "Clara Sharland," is written on the typescript in Savitri Devi's handwriting, lead me to believe that the typescript belonged to Savitri Devi, meaning that Savitri Devi thought enough of the poem to type it out and keep it among her papers for the rest of her life. That fact alone is reason enough to include it in the collection of The Savitri Devi Archive.

I have included it in this volume, however, because there is good reason to think that the author may be Savitri Devi herself. Several facts suggest this. For instance, Savitri did not merely type out Clara Sharland's name as one would normally do when typing a copy of a poem. She "signed" Clara Sharland's name at the end of the poem, as if she herself were the author using a (new) pen name. ("Savitri Devi" was, after all, merely a pen name of Maximine Portaz.)

Although the subject of the poem was very dear to Savitri's heart, and although the sentiments expressed are similar to those of Savitri's known works, these facts alone do not suggest her authorship, for Savitri would not have copied the work of another author if it did not accord with her own interests and sentiments.

But there are also stylistic similarities between this poem and Savitri Devi's other works. First, Savitri was inclined to use dates in the titles of her poems. All sixteen poems in *Forever and Ever* are named for particular years. Second, Savitri was also inclined to capitalize all pronouns referring to Adolf Hitler, much as Christians capitalize pronouns referring to God and Jesus. Third, Savitri was fond of capitalizing significant words that would otherwise be in lower case, and in the poem we find, in the first stanza, "Eagle," "Best," "Highest," and "Land"; in the second, "Eagle"; in the third, "Eagle" and "Dead"; in the fourth, "Angel"; and in the fifth, "Land." Fourth, Savitri was an eccentric punctuator, and one of her characteristic patterns is to combine a comma (and sometimes a semicolon) with a dash, which appears in the fourth and fifth stanzas: "He rests,—at last"; "And fought to guard,—and died."

❖ ❖ ❖

This is not the first time "In Memory of May 1st, 1945" has appeared in print. A version appears, for instance, in the poetry section of the Historical Review Press website.[1] Evidently it has been copied from a print publication.

There are many differences between the typescript and the published version. Some of these differences may simply be errors of transcription, either from the original typescript or from the original printed version to the website. Other differences, however, seem to be the product of a rather heavy editorial hand. For instance, the entire fourth stanza has been eliminated in the published version. A chart comparing the two versions appears on page 110 below. Differences are noted in bold. Notice also the differences in indentation.

The fact that Savitri Devi's typescript contains an extra stanza means that she could not have copied it from the published version. (Assuming, of course, that the website version is substantially the same as the printed version.) This is one more reason to think that she was the author.

According to the Historical Review Press website, the poem was penned by "Clare [not 'Clara'] Sharland, an English woman." The site adds that:

> Her poetic inspiration was awarded First Prize for poems penned on topical events in 1945. Walter de la Mare, English poet, and President of the Poetry Society awarded the prize. Miss Sharland refused the prize, saying: "These words were written in tears and despair. I decided to submit them hoping that they might give a few people at least a glimpse of the other side. Money or anything money will buy, I could not take for them, for money has been the whole cause of this monstrous tragedy.

---

[1] http://www.ety.com/HRP/poetics/may01_1945.htm

My words belong to an entirely other world where money has no weight. I am glad that I have won your prize for the glorious man who made such a magnificent fight to save the world and failed. We praise him in his failure, we praise him in his eternal victory."

The words attributed to the poem's author do not exactly "sound" like Savitri Devi. Savitri, it is true, was always passing up opportunities for financial gain from her writings, so much so that she often became a burden on her friends. It is also true that Savitri frequently contrasted National Socialism to the "international money power," i.e., capitalism and the Jews. But I cannot imagine her saying that "money has been the whole cause of this monstrous tragedy [i.e., the Second World War]."

Thus far, my attempts to trace the original publication of "In Memory of May 1st, 1945" have been in vain. The Poetry Society of which Walter de la Mare (1873–1956) was the president never sponsored a contest or awarded a prize for poems on events in 1945, nor did the poem appear in the society's journal *Poetry Review*. So the contest in question must have been sponsored by another organization. An examination of the papers of Walter de la Mare, if extant, may furnish the necessary lead. If another scholar wishes to pursue this topic, I wish him good luck. I will gladly publish his findings at the Savitri Devi Archive.

❖ ❖ ❖

The case for Savitri Devi's authorship of this poem is still open. Nevertheless, "In Memory of May 1st, 1945" is a small but significant acquisition for the Savitri Devi Archive, whether it ultimately belongs among Savitri Devi's works or merely among her papers.

COMPARISON OF TWO VERSIONS

Typescript version:

Great Eagle, fold your wings awhile
  And turn away your eyes;
In smoke and thunder, flame and blood
   Your **Best** and **Highest** dies;
   And all **His** happy Land,
    His great **emprise,**
A shattered wreck of ugly ruin lies.

Great Eagle, flee a little while
   To some far lonely height.
   There shall you watch and wait...
   Your land is sunk in night:
   All, all those cities bright
In ruins far and wide torment the night.

Oh Eagle, did you hear that shout,
   That thundered triple roar?
Its **clamourous** echoes smote the earth,
   And rolled from shore to shore;
   And all the glorious **Dead,**
   Who fealty swore,
Received **Him** home; **His** earthly flight is o'er.

His fight, that made the nations shake,
   And hearts and pulses leap,
   Is over now. He rests. But we
   Are sunk in anguish deep.
   He rests,—at last. No dreams
   Torture His sleep,
While grave-eyed Angel-guards their watches keep.

Great Eagle, that **He** worked to save,
   And fought to guard,—and died,
Flee **from** this piteous German wreck,
   In some far corner hide,
   Until **the** Land is free
   And far and wide,
Throughout the world **His** name is glorified!

Meanwhile, *we* hold the heights **He** won,
   And keep **His** torch aflame;
No slothful ease for us who bear
   The honour of **His** name.
   To do **His** work we count
   Higher than fame,
Indifferent to earthly praise or **blame.**

Clara Sharland

Historical Review Press version:

Great Eagle, fold your wings awhile,
And turn away your eyes.
In smoke and thunder, flame and blood,
Your best and highest dies;
And all his happy land,
His great **demise**
A shattered wreck of ugly ruin lies.

Great Eagle, flee a little while,
To some far lonely height.
There shall you watch and wait.
Your land is sunk in night
For all those cities bright,
In ruins far and wide torment the night.

Great Eagle, did you hear that shout—
That thundered triple roar?
Its clamorous echoes smote the earth,

And all the glorious dead
Who fealty swore,
Received him home; his earthly fight is o'er.

Great Eagle, that he worked to save,
And fought to guard—and died;
Flee this piteous German wreck.
In some far corner hide
Until **thy** land is free;
And far and wide throughout the world,
His name is glorified.

Meanwhile **we** hold the heights he won,
And keep his torch aflame.
No slothful ease for us who bear
The honour of his name.
To do his work we count
Higher than fame,
Indifferent to **mere** earthly praise or **flame.**

Clare Sharland

INDEX

ABOUT THE AUTHORESS

SAVITRI DEVI (1905–1982) is one of the most original and influential National Socialist thinkers of the post-World War II era. Born Maximine Julia Portaz in Lyons, France on 30 September 1905, she was of English, Greek, and Italian ancestry and described her nationality as "Indo-European." She earned Master's Degrees in philosophy and chemistry and a Ph.D. in philosophy from the University of Lyons.

A self-described "nationalist of every nation" and an Indo-European pagan revivalist, Savitri Devi embraced National Socialism in 1929 while in Palestine. In 1935, she traveled to India to experience in Hinduism the last living Indo-European pagan religion. Settling eventually in Calcutta, she worked for the Hindu nationalist movement, married a Bengali Brahmin, the pro-Axis publisher Asit Krishna Mukherji, and spied for the Japanese during World War II.

After World War II, Savitri Devi embarked upon an itinerant, ascetic life. Her two chief activities were tirelessly witnessing on behalf of National Socialism and caring for homeless and abused animals.

Savitri Devi influenced such leading figures of post-war National Socialism as George Lincoln Rockwell, Colin Jordan, William Pierce, and Miguel Serrano. In 1962, she took part in the Cotswolds camp, where the World Union of National Socialists (WUNS) was formed.

Her books include *A Warning to the Hindus* (1939), *L'Etang aux lotus* (*The Lotus Pond*) (1940), *A Son of God: The Life and Philosophy of Akhnaton, King of Egypt* (1946), later republished as *Son of the Sun* (1956), *Akhnaton: A Play* (1948), *Defiance: The Prison Memoirs of Savitri Devi* (1951), *Gold in the Furnace: Experiences in Post-War Germany* (1952), *The Lightning and the Sun* (1958), *Pilgrimage* (1958), *Impeachment of Man* (1959), *Long-Whiskers and the Two-Legged Goddess* (1965), *Souvenirs et réflexions d'une Aryenne* (*Memories and Reflections of an Aryan Woman*) (1976), and *And Time Rolls On: The Savitri Devi Interviews* (2005).

Savitri Devi died in Sible Hedingham, Essex, England on 22 October 1982, at the age of 77.

www.ingramcontent.com/pod-product-compliance
Lightning Source LLC
Chambersburg PA
CBHW020205090426
42734CB00008B/950